ALL-TIME GREATEST BASKETBALL STORIES FOR KIDS

15 LEGENDARY HOOPS JOURNEYS, LIFE LESSONS, AND HEROIC ATHLETES TO INSPIRE YOUNG READERS TO OVERCOME CHALLENGES AND FOLLOW THEIR DREAMS

CHRIS VILLANUEVA

CONTENTS

INTRODUCTION

Imagine it's a cold, snowy winter, and you have nothing fun to do. You have an awesome teacher who wants to help make sure you and your classmates still make fun memories together. He grabs a soccer ball and two peach baskets and hangs the peach baskets on the wall. The goal is to score the soccer ball into the two peach baskets. You have two teams of nine helping each other score the ball while the other team tries to stop you. You have a ton of fun playing this game, which teaches you many incredible lessons. The winter months seem to fly by.

This is what happened a long time ago in Springfield, Mass-achusetts. The inventor of basketball, James Naismith, was a teacher just like the ones you have at school. He only wanted to keep his students active during the cold winter months. It may have started out as just another fun game. Yet, he ended up creating something that would capture the hearts of people around the world and inspire millions to chase their dreams and overcome challenges.

As a young reader, you probably have things you think a lot about. Maybe you're worried about that test at school next week, trying to get better at a hobby, or what you want to be when you grow up. You may need help staying motivated and believing in yourself. Guess what? Every kid faces challenges, just like the basketball legends in this book. It's not easy trying to figure out who you are and have confidence in yourself. But we're not meant to figure everything out on our own. We need stories and role models to show us how to become our best version.

Here's some great news—you have so much potential because you're a young reader. You have the power to build whatever life you want for yourself. Maybe you chose to start reading this book, or perhaps someone special gave it to you because they believe in you. The point is that you are in the perfect position to learn some life-changing lessons. Lessons that teach you courage, hard work, and the joy of achieving your goals.

This book was written to tell you stories about some of the most incredible basketball players ever. These players might seem like superhumans, but the reality is that they started out as young kids, too. They went through their own struggles, obstacles, and victories. They have unique stories about how they found basketball and made it their passion. Parents, teachers, and coaches love sharing stories like these because they're not just about basketball—they're also about life.

As we dive into these stories together, you'll be inspired by what these players were able to overcome. You'll discover how to tackle tough times with a smile, believe in yourself even when things get hard, and work with your friends to make every game a win. You'll see how sharing these stories can bring you closer to your family, friends, and teammates—turning reading time into bonding time.

But there's more! This book is a treasure chest, and inside, you'll find more wisdom on:

- Sticking to it, even when it starts to get tough
- Building confidence to reach for the stars
- Creating habits that help you succeed
- Understanding others and working together as a team
- Finding the courage to chase your dreams in sports and beyond
- Enjoying special moments with the people you love
- Seeing the world in new ways and making your mark
- Falling in love with reading, learning, and growing every day

By the end of this book, you'll see a brighter, more exciting world where anything is possible when you put your heart into it. You'll be inspired to dribble past doubts, shoot for your goals, and score your dreams.

It's absolutely okay if basketball does not become your passion or you still need to figure out what you want to do. In the end, I'm here to share these stories because I believe in the power of dreams and the strength inside each and every one of you. This book not only shows you how to become a great basketball player, it also shows you how to become great at anything you decide to do.

Also, reading is meant to be fun and educational. This book is a great blend of both, where we take time to walk you through each person's story and tie it all together with the lessons we can take away from it. At the end of each chapter, we allow you to discuss the lessons and reflect on your life with your parents, teacher, or coaches. Remember, you can learn a lot from them, too—so don't skip this step and make sure you talk to them.

So, are you ready to jump into a world where basketball and life lessons come together? A world where every turn of the page reveals a new secret to bring out your best self? Get fired up, and let's start this incredible journey together. You, too, can achieve all-time greatness.

CHAPTER ONE

MAGIC AND BIRD: THE RIVALRY THAT TRANSFORMED THE NBA

"We cared about winning the game and making our teammates better. That's why we were able to change not only basketball but also the NBA."

—MAGIC JOHNSON (ON HIMSELF AND LARRY BIRD)

Basketball is a competitive game. While you should always strive to have fun, the main goal when you play basketball is to win the game. You want your team to score more points than your opponents. You hope to play better than other people. Competing against a friend or rival makes you more motivated to win. Who doesn't want to beat their friend in a game? This type of friendly competition makes both of you even better players. In this chapter, we'll learn about Magic and Larry, who became legendary players individually thanks to their rivalry. Together, Magic and Larry would elevate the game of basketball across the world.

Magic (Earvin) Johnson and Larry Bird, two basketball legends, grew up in two completely different worlds. Magic grew up in the busy city of Lansing, Michigan. Raised in a neighborhood filled with challenges, he learned the value of hard work and determination from a young age. His dazzling smile and charming personality made him very popular among his friends and community.

On the other hand, Larry hailed from the small town of French Lick, Indiana. Surrounded by nature and farmland, he practiced his skills while shooting baskets in a barn. His family didn't have much money and went through several unfortunate events, so Larry would turn to basketball as his safe place to escape the troubles. To this day, Larry credits his tough childhood with motivating him to keep working hard.

Despite their different childhoods, they both followed their passions for basketball and became good enough to play in college. Their paths collided while they were playing basketball in the NCAA (National College Athletics Association). Magic was a star at Michigan State University, and Larry was a standout at Indiana State. They clashed in the 1979 NCAA Championship game. It was a showdown that captivated the nation. Both were the brightest stars on their teams, competing their hardest, trying to bring their team to victory. Magic's team emerged victorious, but this was just the beginning of their many legendary battles.

The next step for them would be the highest level of professional basketball—the National Basketball Association (NBA). When they entered the NBA, Magic Johnson was drafted by the Los Angeles Lakers and Larry Bird by the Boston Celtics. The Lakers and the Celtics had already met many times in the NBA Finals, and when Magic and Larry became the new stars of these teams, it only intensified their personal rivalry. A rivalry is when two or more people compete against each other for a long time. Magic's Lakers and Larry's Celtics faced off in the NBA Finals multiple times during the 1980s, creating one of the greatest sports rivalries of all time. Magic's fast-paced, flashy style would battle Larry's precision and basketball IQ, making every game a spectacle.

The NBA had never seen such fierce competition. It wasn't just about winning; it was about the artistry of the game. Their battles on the court were more than matches; they were epic stories that unfolded every season. The Lakers and Celtics became the symbol of basketball excellence, capturing the imagination of fans world-wide. Magic and Larry would constantly keep an eye on each other so they would know what their rival was doing and how to beat them. Larry has even said, "The first thing I would do every morning during the season was look at the box scores to see what Magic did."

Magic and Larry's impact on the NBA extended beyond the court. Before they joined the league, the NBA needed help in terms of popularity. There weren't as many fans back then, and people were not interested in this basketball league. Because of Magic and Larry, things began to turn around, and they helped turn the league into the global sensation it is today. Kids everywhere were imitating their moves, trying to replicate the no-look passes of Magic or Larry's deadly three-pointers. The NBA went from a popular American pastime to a global phenomenon thanks to the charisma and skill of these two icons. They began the rise that future stars like Michael Jordan, LeBron James, and Steph Curry would multiply.

By the time they had retired, Magic and Larry were legends for their teams. The both of them had played against each other in the NBA Finals three times, with Magic winning two out of the three. Both of them would win other championships, with Magic having five and Larry having three, with many more accomplishments on top of that. While both were absolutely amazing as individuals, you can't talk about the history of the NBAs in the 1980s without mentioning them and their rivalry.

LESSONS FROM MAGIC JOHNSON AND LARRY BIRD

Their rivalry wasn't just about winning championships; it was about pushing each other to new heights and elevating the sport they loved. Magic and Larry showed everyone that basketball wasn't just a game; it was a canvas for creativity, teamwork, and storytelling. The excitement they brought to the NBA set a new standard, and fans couldn't get enough.

Magic and Larry showed us that competition is not something meant to tear you down or something to be afraid of. In fact, it's the opposite—competition helps make you a better version of yourself. Their battles weren't about hurting each other. Instead, they were like races where each wanted to run faster, jump higher, and score more points. It was healthy competition, two friends and rivals challenging each other to be their best.

Imagine playing a game with your friends. While it can get intense trying to beat each other, you should end up having even more fun and building stronger friendships. That's what a healthy rivalry should do. Magic and Larry did just that. They made basketball a big playground where everyone wanted to play their part, have fun, and win, making the game more exciting for everyone watching.

Even though they were rivals on the court, Magic and Larry taught us about something magical—mutual respect. Mutual respect means that no matter what happened on the court between Magic and Larry, they would still appreciate and congratulate each other on their wins, no matter how angry or intense they might have gotten. Larry knew Magic was special because of his flashy passes, and Magic knew Larry's incredible shooting was deadly. They appreciated that about each other. They showed us that it's okay to compete fiercely but still be kind and supportive, like teammates in the game of life.

Think about playing your favorite sport with your friends. You might be on different teams, but deep down, everyone's goal is to have fun and perform well. Magic and Larry were like that; even in the heat of competition, they respected each other's talents and hard work. It's like having a great friend you can count on, even when trying your hardest to win.

Their rivalry wasn't just about who could make better passes or three-point shots; it was about being good sports. That means shaking hands after a game, saying, "Good job!" even if you didn't win, and understanding that everyone is learning and growing. That's called sportsmanship. Sportsmanship means you still treat your opponents and rivals with respect and fairness. Magic and Bird were the perfect examples of how competition and sportsmanship can create unforgettable moments.

So, when you play your favorite games with friends, remember the lessons from Magic and Larry. Embrace healthy competition, where everyone pushes each other to be their best and always shares a dose of mutual respect and sportsmanship. When you do this, you will enjoy the game much more. This goes beyond just games; it applies to any competitions you find in real life; you'll definitely run into a few!

Magic and Bird also had this incredible power called the competitive spirit. Picture yourself at the starting line as you enter a race with your friend. You adore your friends, but you must win this, or else they get bragging rights. Victory is the only option here. As the race begins, you are running fast but then notice your friend is running just a little faster. So you pick up the pace and put in even more effort than you imagined, and so does your friend. As the race nears the end, you are both running faster than you each thought possible. You win the race! Not only did you win the race, but you also ran faster than you thought you could. That's what a healthy competition does for you. It pushes you further and improves you. The next time you find yourself in a competition, although it might add stress to the situation, remember it can push you to new levels.

Imagine you have a friend who's really good at building LEGO towers. Instead of feeling jealous of their skills, you can be inspired to build an even cooler tower. That's what Magic and Bird did in basketball. They were friendly but were always trying to outdo each other in a game of hoops. But here's the secret: instead of feeling sad when the other did well, they used it as superpower fuel to become even better. So, when you see a friend doing awesome stuff, let it spark your own magic and motivate you to reach for the stars.

Magic and Bird had the most intense of competitions, but they always stayed respectful and supportive of each other. There was no Magic without Bird, and no Bird without Magic. They showed us that even in the heat of a game, you can be super respectful to your buddies. Don't let the heat or intensity of competition take you away from the beauty of the game. Everyone is out there trying to have fun and do their best. This goes beyond sports. If you are an astronaut, firefighter, scientist, or doctor, you will find others competing in the same field. Remember, this is great for you and will push you to be better; remember to enjoy the journey and be respectful of others.

Magic Johnson and Larry Bird are two NBA legends who helped turn the NBA from a struggling league to one of the most popular sports across the world. They went through many tough battles against each other, but the result was that they both became even better players and leaders for their teams. Everyone, including themselves, benefited from the competition.

ACTIVITY

Take some time to answer these questions, and invite an adult to help you.

- Have you ever had a rivalry or competition that pushed you to do better? If yes, what was that experience like?
- Think about the last time you lost. Did you show sportsmanship to your opponents?
- Think of someone who challenges you to do better. Write down ways to learn from them and maintain a positive and respectful relationship.

CHAPTER TWO

MICHAEL JORDAN: THE MAN WHO FLEW

"I've failed over and over and over again in my life. And that is why I succeed."

—MICHAEL JORDAN

B asketball is a team game, but certain players are considered some of the greatest to ever play. If you ask your parents or teachers, they might say Michael Jordan was the greatest player to ever play basketball. Before Michael Jordan became a global icon and known as the greatest player of all time, he was just another kid. His early life was marked by humble beginnings and a gradual rise similar to anyone else's. Born in Brooklyn, New York, in 1963, he moved to North Carolina while still a young boy. That was where his journey to basketball greatness began.

Michael had an older brother, Larry, who greatly influenced his life. Michael says Larry was an incredible mentor to him when he grew up. Larry loved basketball, and he spread that love to his younger brother, Michael. At first, Michael just wanted to impress his brother and spend time with him. They would play together in their backyard, shooting jump shots, playing one-on-one, and having fun as kids. Little did they know, these moments would become the seeds of greatness for Michael.

Michael kept playing the game. Throughout middle school, his love for basketball grew like a flourishing plant. By the time he got into high school at Emsley A. Laney High, North Carolina, it was clear that Michael's basketball gifts were beginning to show. But even then, Michael faced a tough moment when he tried out for his high school varsity basketball team but did not make the cut. He wasn't let into the team. It was a big, disappointing bump in his basketball journey.

It can really hurt to be rejected, especially if it's for something you love to do. That's what happened to Michael Jordan in high school. It hurt, but Michael did not give up. Instead, he joined the junior varsity team, a level below where he wanted to play, and worked to prove himself from there. Instead of feeling sad and sorry for himself, he decided to try even harder.

Michael chose to not give up. He joined the junior varsity team, practiced like crazy, and guess what?—he made it to the varsity team and became the star player. It's like when you fall off your bike—you get back on and try again. This time, instead of falling off the bike, you figure out how to ride it fast down the road. That's the first big lesson from Michael's story—never give up, even if things don't go how you want or don't go how you planned. Setbacks don't need to stop you; they might make the journey longer, but the treasure is worth it.

Michael's skills caught the eye of college scouts, and he got a scholarship to the University of North Carolina (UNC). A scholarship is when a college will pay for your education so you can play basketball for them. College was the next big step for Michael toward his goal of making it to the NBA. Challenges would always keep coming, but he did not let anything stop him. Really good high school players continue to play college basketball in the NCAA. In 1982, during the NCAA Championship game, Michael made a shot that would go down in history. He scored the winning basket with just seconds left on the game clock, helping UNC become champions. It was the kind of joyous moment he would have never forgotten. To think this is the same kid who got cut from his high school varsity team.

Michael would continue to have a great college career. The NBA, the ultimate professional basketball league, would be Michael's amazing next step. In 1984, the Chicago Bulls picked him in the draft as the third overall pick. Suddenly, Michael was in a whole new world of even fiercer competition. But this was his chance to shine, and shine he did.

Michael's impact was felt from the moment he stepped onto an NBA court. He won the NBA Rookie of the Year award, meaning he was the best out of all the new players who joined that year. It was showing everyone that the kid from Wilmington had something special. The Bulls, who were once struggling, started winning because of Michael's incredible talent and leadership. Michael became known for his ability to jump high and dunk the ball in unique ways. People around the world would call him "Air Jordan."

Success took hard work for Michael. In his early years, the Detroit Pistons stood in the way of Michael and the Chicago Bulls winning championships. They were an incredible team at the time, known for their rough and brutal play style. It was like climbing a steep mountain, but Michael was super determined. Year after year, he practiced harder, played smarter, and led his team with passion.

In 1991, the breakthrough came. Michael and the Bulls won their first NBA Championship. It was a dream come true for Michael, who had faced many challenges along the way. But this was just the beginning. The Bulls went on to win two more repeating championships in 1992 and 1993, establishing themselves as an NBA dynasty. They were a scary team that people had trouble beating.

In 1993, Michael shocked the world by retiring from basketball at the peak of his success. He felt so physically and mentally exhausted from the difficult journey of winning his championships. It was an insanely tough moment for fans, as he was the most popular basketball player in the world. During his time away from the game, Michael explored baseball, another sport he loved as a kid. However, the basketball court's pull was strong, and in 1995, he made a triumphant return to the NBA after he found his passion again.

This comeback story was magical. Even though Michael was gone for two years, he returned to lead the Bulls to three more repeating championships in 1996, 1997, and 1998. It was like he never left. There was no stopping him. This became the legacy that Michael established in the NBA. Every little kid adored him. He had fans coming to watch him from all over the world.

When Michael retired, he had six NBA Championships, five Most Valuable Player (MVP) awards, led the league in scoring in ten different seasons, earned one Defensive Player of the Year award, and many more. His list of accomplishments is amazing, but even more impressive is that he made basketball a more popular sport worldwide. Michael had more fans than any other player in NBA history, inspiring a generation of new basketball stars to play after him. He captured the imagination of what was possible on the basketball court. He was exceptional and is known by many as the greatest basketball player of all time.

LESSONS FROM MICHAEL JORDAN

Knowing these wins weren't just handed to Michael is an important lesson. He had to practice and put in the work. Imagine playing your favorite video game or riding a bike—the more you do it, the better you get. It's the same with many things in life, including basketball. Although Michael might seem like a super-hero who would fly across the basketball court, he did not become that overnight. He practiced hard so that he could become better. You don't become the greatest without practice.

Even when he was already really good, Michael didn't stop. He dribbled, practiced shooting, and worked on his moves every single day. The more you repeat something, the better you get. The practice may become boring and draining because you repeat something so many times. Still, Michael always knew that this was the key to becoming a great player.

So, when things get tough, remember Michael Jordan's story. Keep going, even if you don't win the first time. Practice like it's your superpower, and soon, you'll be scoring your slam dunks in the game of life.

Michael taught about the power of resilience. Resilience is how he was always able to bounce back and practice harder, even after losing and failing. Resilience means you can come back from hard times and keep going. When he was cut from his varsity team or when the Detroit Pistons kept beating him, he stayed resilient and kept trying to do better. That's what helped him become this basketball legend everyone talks about. So, when things don't go your way, remember to be like Michael—shake it off, stand tall, and keep soaring.

He taught us the power of work ethic. Like Michael, hard work should be your secret potion. Practice like a champ, not just when you start but even when you are already the best. Be consistent. Don't just work hard only once or just for a few days; work hard for many months and years. So, when you want to get better at something, remember to put in the work. It's like planting seeds—the more you water and care for them, the bigger they grow. This is the key to success in all you do.

Michael Jordan didn't just aim for the hoop; he had big dreams and set goals to make them happen. Imagine you want to score ten points in your next game. That's the goal—an achievable one. Break down your big dreams into smaller steps—like building blocks. Each block is a small goal that leads to your big victory. It's like building the coolest LEGO castle, one piece at a time.

Short-term goals are like checkpoints in a race. Say you want to be the fastest runner in your class. Set a short-term goal to improve your running time every week. Celebrate each small victory, such as when you shorten your running time every second or minute. Each step is one step closer to your goal. Picture yourself achieving your goals, which will help you make them come true.

If you stumble, remember that our role models face tough days, too. Michael Jordan didn't win every game; he faced failures. It's okay to fail sometimes. Use it as fuel to try even harder next time. Learn from mistakes, just like leveling up in a game. It gives you experience and builds up your confidence. Remember, it's not about how many times you fall. It's about how many times you get back up. The key is to stay positive and remind yourself that you can do it.

Michael Jordan's journey teaches us about facing struggles, never giving up, and reaching for the stars. He became more than a basketball player; he became an icon—a symbol of resilience and excellence. Kids everywhere can look up to Michael Jordan and learn that they can overcome obstacles and achieve their dreams with determination and hard work. And so, the story of Michael Jordan, the kid who rose from setbacks to become a basketball legend, continues to inspire us all.

So, future champions, be like Michael—resilient, hardworking, goal-setters, and fearless in the face of failure. Your story is just beginning, and you're the hero who gets to write it.

Don't forget: with your dreams in sight, practice with all your might, face challenges light—in life's flight, be like Mike.

ACTIVITY

Take some time to answer these questions, and invite an adult to help you.

- Think about a time when you failed or were rejected. Did you get back up and try again? Can you commit to being resilient? Just like when Michael did not give up after being cut from his varsity team?
- Think about something you want to get better at. Set a personal goal this week to work on it, no matter how small. Start somewhere. Please write down the steps you'll take to achieve it.

CHAPTER THREE

KOBE BRYANT: THE MAMBA MENTALITY

"The most important thing is to try and inspire people so that they can be great at whatever they want to do."

—KOBE BRYANT

There is a legendary player in NBA history who has invented a way of life. He invented a mindset that millions of people apply in their own lives—a mindset of excellence and dedication. He used this mindset to do incredible things on the basketball court and draw the hearts and minds of fans around the world. This mindset is the Mamba Mentality, created by the Black Mamba himself, Kobe Bryant.

Kobe Bean Bryant was born in Philadelphia, Pennsylvania. His dad was former NBA player Joe Bryant. When Kobe was six years old, his father retired from the NBA after eight seasons. He moved to Italy to continue his career in basketball overseas. Kobe was used to moving around Italy because of his dad and actually learned to speak fluent Italian. It was there he joined a youth basketball league and started playing competitive basketball.

When Kobe was thirteen years old, his family moved back to the United States of America, where he attended Lower Merion High School. As a first-year student, he played on the varsity team, which is very impressive for someone that age. As a third-year student, he was named Philadelphia Player of the Year. Kobe became the all-time scoring leader for his school in history, beating even Wilt Chamberlain's record at 2883 points, and led Lower Merion to their first State Championship in fifty-three years.

When Kobe was about to finish high school, he received scholarship offers from nearly every major college. Still, he decided to reject all of them. So, instead of going to college, he declared himself for the 1996 NBA Draft, where he was drafted by the Charlotte Hornets with the thirteenth pick. He was immediately traded to the Los Angeles Lakers for starting center Vlade Divac. He became the youngest NBA player in history when the 1996–97 season began.

During a workout, Kobe completely dominated former NBA players Michael Cooper and Larry Drew, causing Jerry West, the Lakers general manager, to notice him. At this time, one of the most dominant stars in the NBA, Shaquille O'Neal, had also been signed by the Lakers, and the two would soon form one of the NBA's most dominant duos ever.

Kobe served as a reserve behind Eddie Jones and Nick Van Exel for his first two seasons. Being the youngest player to play in an NBA game and still with a lot to prove, he had limited playing time early on. Kobe played for six minutes, without scoring any points, against the Minnesota Timberwolves. He scored his first point in the NBA with a free throw in a game against the New York Knicks.

As the season continued, Kobe received more playing time and, on January 28, became the youngest player in the starting lineup for a game in which the Lakers won over the Dallas Mavericks. Kobe won the 1997 Slam Dunk Championship during All-Star weekend and earned an NBA Rookie Second Team selection for his performance throughout the season.

In 1999, Phil Jackson became the Lakers' coach, with Shaq as a center and Kobe as the shooting guard. Kobe and Shaq formed a deadly one-two punch, where Kobe would take over games with his deadly scoring ability, and Shaq would control the paint with his unstoppable strength. The Lakers would dominate the league and win three consecutive NBA Championships between 2000–02. The streak would end as Kobe and Shaq experienced some personal difficulties and were defeated in the second round of the 2003 playoffs. After another loss in the 2004 finals, Shaq was traded, so Kobe became the sole leader of the Lakers.

Kobe led the league in scoring during the 2005–06 and 2006–07 seasons and was named MVP in 2008 for the first time in his career. In 2009, Kobe won his fourth NBA Championship and was named the Finals MVP after scoring an average of 32.4 points per game in the series. He led the Lakers to their third consecutive Western Conference Championship in 2009–10. He was once more named the MVP of the NBA Finals after the Lakers defeated the Boston Celtics in a dramatic seven-game series that went down to the wire.

One of Kobe's many nicknames is the Black Mamba. He created an alter ego during one of the hardest times of his life. He explained that the Mamba Mentality means "just trying to get better every day." In his autobiography, *The Mamba Mentality*, Kobe discusses the power of obsession.

"If you want to be great in a particular area, you have to obsess over it. A lot of people say they want to be great, but they're not willing to make the sacrifices necessary to achieve greatness. They have other concerns, whether important or not, and they spread themselves out." This is one of his more famous statements.

During tough times in his life, when Kobe would feel down or lose sight of himself, he could always turn to his alter ego, "The Black Mamba," as a force with a powerful competitive spirit and intense work ethic, reminding himself to always strive to be the best version of himself and give his best effort in everything he did.

This mentality would take Kobe to incredible heights and accomplishments. Throughout his twenty-year NBA career, Kobe earned eighteen All-Star selections, five NBA Championship titles, two NBA Finals MVP awards, and two Olympic gold medals. Outside of basketball, Kobe published several books, gave back to the community, was head of his own studio, and was the father of four girls. Although he had a lot of talent, his colleagues have agreed that Kobe had one of the most determined and toughest mindsets of any individual on earth. Despite Kobe no longer being with us, the Mamba Mentality lives on in the hearts and minds of millions of people.

LESSONS FROM KOBE BRYANT

Firstly, Kobe was both a student and a master of the game. He denied himself many things to focus on being the best, always determined to lead his team to victory. Kobe had a very disciplined work ethic. Sure, he had a lot of talent, but he wasn't the fastest, strongest, or most talented player of his time. What, then, made him the best? His dedication to be the best. Dedication means you're not just thinking about it but also waking up every day and choosing to put in the work to achieve your dreams.

Kobe's dedication to mastery meant he worked harder and gave more effort than anyone around him. He approached challenges as an opportunity to learn and improve yourself. He chose to fight for dreams instead of living with regrets for not being more talented than the next guy. Kobe took his defeats and failures and turned them into successes. There was a time when Kobe played a game left-handed when an injured shoulder did not allow him to shoot with his right hand. In another game, he even played with a 102-degree fever to make sure his team would get the win. He never let himself make excuses.

It might be easy to point to masters like Kobe and remark on their God-given talent. Still, it would be wise to acknowledge all the hard work and discipline that made them who they are. What differentiates an ordinary player from an extraordinary one is the amount of time, work, and dedication they put into perfecting the craft. Kobe understood this perfectly and often practiced it in his daily life. Even when he was great, he wanted to be better.

He was often the first to turn up for practice. He sometimes even showed up despite having minor injuries. He would regularly begin practice as early as 4 a.m., refusing to leave until he had made hundreds and hundreds of shots. He often demanded his teammates show the same level of commitment and competitiveness that he did. Sometimes, it made him a harsh leader since he pushed others so hard, but in the long run, it benefited them.

In addition to mastery, Kobe talks about the importance of failure. Failure is inevitable and, when done right, can teach you precious lessons about improvement. Kobe understood that failing at first was a part of the process of learning something new. You must be willing to do your best despite failing and be prepared to get up and try again. Do not be afraid of embarrassing yourself, and strive for continuous improvement. This is what leads to mental toughness and resilience.

Resilience is the ability to recover quickly from difficulties or being tough. Kobe never let himself be kept down by anything—not illness, tiredness, or other people's opinions. He had a goal and worked toward it with unwavering focus. Whenever you face a difficult challenge, you can ask yourself, "What would Kobe do?" Would he give up, or would he push through? Would he find another way to achieve his goal? Would he shoot left-handed if he needed to?

To apply the Mamba Mentality, you have to first set a goal. A goal is a result you want to achieve. It could be anything from what you want to be in the future or what grade you want on your next test. A good goal is something that pushes you. For example, if you are currently a C or B student, your goal should not be to get a C or B on your next test but to get an A. If you are an A student, your goal would be to get an A+ or 100 percent on the next test. Ensure you set goals that take you out of your comfort zone and push you to improve.

To set an ambitious goal, you should first determine its purpose. What do you want to feel when you achieve it, or why do you want to achieve it? Do you want an award or to make your parents proud? For instance, you want to run a mile in less than ten minutes to become more athletic and have a better chance of doing well in sports. Take that goal and break it into small chunks. This week, try to run a mile in less than twenty minutes or a half mile in less than ten minutes. Once you accomplish that, decrease the time you are going for. Continue this every week for a month and mark how much your running speed improves.

There will be obstacles to your goal, but you must devise a way to overcome them. Some common obstacles can be wanting more energy or blaming the weather. You should treat your goal as an important thing in your life and make time for it. Don't let yourself come up with excuses that distract you from it.

Do not be afraid to embrace your inner mamba. It may take time to see results, but consistency is key. Start small and build on it every day, and you will start noticing changes in how you handle problems. Be mentally tough like Kobe.

ACTIVITY

Take some time to answer these questions, and invite an adult to help you.

- Has there been a time recently that you let an excuse stop you from an important task?
- Think of a challenging goal. What steps can you take to achieve it with the Mamba Mentality?
- Identify a skill or area you want to improve in. Create a plan for working on it consistently, drawing inspiration from Kobe's dedication to practice and improvement.

CHAPTER FOUR

LEBRON JAMES: THE KING OF BASKETBALL

"You can't be afraid to fail. It's the only way to succeed."

—LEBRON JAMES

Nobody believed Michael Jordan could be challenged as the greatest player ever. Only when another basketball legend showed up in 2003 did that belief change. A legend who would be able to play at a superstar level and be the face of the league for more than twenty years and counting. A legend who continues to defy belief and break all-time records. That player is LeBron James.

The fantastic story of LeBron James begins in a little town called Akron, Ohio. He had a rough childhood, where his father left him, and he only grew up with his mother, Gloria. They barely had any money and even had to rely on coupons to have enough food. Because of this, LeBron didn't have all the fancy things other kids had. Because they had to move around a lot and his mom had to work multiple jobs to provide enough food, LeBron spent some time living with his local football coach when he was nine.

This coach, Frankie Walker, introduced LeBron to basketball so that he wouldn't fall for the bad influences in the streets of Akron. It was immediately obvious that LeBron had a natural talent for basketball, and his love for it bloomed on the courts of Akron. He'd spend hours practicing his dribbling and shooting, dreaming of becoming a basketball star one day. Despite the hardships, his mom was his biggest supporter, cheering him on from the sidelines. LeBron's determination grew stronger. A lot of credit for helping LeBron find his passion is owed to his childhood coach.

He attended Riedinger Middle School, where he began elevating his basketball skills. Even back then, everyone could see he had something special. LeBron was tall and athletic even when he was a kid, and he used this to his advantage on the court. Imagine a ten-year-old kid moving through the concrete grounds, his sneakers screeching, scoring easily like a grown man playing with kids. He was exceptional. His friends and family noticed his special talent, and every single time, they sat in the bleachers, cheering him on during games at the local community center.

Later, he continued his basketball journey at St. Vincent–St. Mary High School. This was where everybody began to notice LeBron's amazing talent. At this time, he was six foot three and wasn't just good; he was like a basketball prodigy, scoring points and making incredible plays that amazed everyone. He was gradually becoming a basketball sensation. Kids, parents, and coaches from all over the country would soon come to watch him play, and he led his high school team to incredible wins. LeBron was like a superhero on the court, just without the cape and with dunking and scoring finesse.

LeBron's favorite player was Michael Jordan, and he dreamed of becoming a basketball superstar just like him. So he learned to practice, just like him. He became the captain of his team, and he began to do almost everything. He would become a great leader, like a football quarterback, passing the ball to teammates with precision. He would move so quickly and jump so high to slam incredible dunks. He learned how to become a great scorer like Michael Jordan but also impressed everyone with his ability to make plays for his teammates. He was a complete and well-rounded basketball player.

As LeBron grew older, his skills on the court became more and more impressive. He became stronger and faster. By the time he finished playing for his high school team, he had led them to three State Championships and was named "Mr. Basketball" in Ohio for three straight years. That's where the nickname "King James" came from because he was like royalty on the basketball court. Everyone admired the skills of this young boy. Little did he know his incredible journey had just begun.

LeBron was so good in high school that he was already being scouted by the NBA. Like Kobe, LeBron was so good that he didn't even need to go to college. His dream had been to play alongside Michael Jordan in the big leagues. Not only did he get drafted, but he was also chosen as the first overall pick in the NBA draft by the Cleveland Cavaliers, his hometown team. Cleveland was just a few miles away from Akron, where he grew up. It was mind-blowing—a dream come true for young LeBron, the hometown hero, and he was ready to show the world what he could do.

His journey to the NBA was a fairytale. It was just 2003, and being the first overall draft pick by the Cleveland Cavaliers meant everybody was going to be watching him closely. But LeBron impressed each time. He wasn't just a basketball player; he was a phenomenon. His skills were jaw-dropping, and he took the Cavaliers to new heights, making fans all over the world. He became known for his incredible dunks, precise passes, and unique ability to score points and consistently win games in the most thrilling ways. No one could do it like LeBron.

His journey in the NBA was challenging. He faced tough opponents and had to work hard to win games. They would consistently make the playoffs in his first seven seasons with the Cleveland Cavaliers. Still, he would fail to win a championship, losing to great teams like the Boston Celtics. He wouldn't give up on his dream to win an NBA Championship.

LeBron's journey continued when he joined the Miami Heat in 2010, where he would win two NBA Championships in 2012 and 2013. Although people didn't like that he left his hometown team, he decided to do what was best for him. But fans wouldn't stay mad forever because LeBron returned to the Cleveland Cavaliers and won their first ever NBA Championship in 2016, beating the legendary Golden State Warriors. Finally, years later, he took his talents to the Los Angeles Lakers, where he would win another NBA Championship, becoming a legend for multiple teams, something few players ever do.

LeBron James continued to amaze everyone with his basketball skills, and he didn't just play for himself; he played for his teammates and the fans who believed in him. As the years went by, LeBron's legacy grew. He became one of the greatest basketball players of all time, breaking records and achieving remarkable feats. He currently has four NBA Championships and four NBA MVPs, holds the record for the most points scored in a single player's career, and is still going strong after playing more than twenty years in the NBA. Ever since 2003, he has been the face of the league. When people think of the NBA, they think of LeBron James. More than that, he remained humble and kind, reminding everyone that greatness comes not only from talent—but also from being a good-hearted individual.

LESSONS FROM LEBRON JAMES

The story of LeBron James has become an inspiration for kids everywhere. It shows them that with hard work, perseverance, and a big dream, they, too, can achieve greatness on the courts of their lives. He became a basketball sensation not only known for his powerful dunks and superstar skills on the court but also someone who teaches us valuable lessons about teamwork, leadership, and making a positive impact in our communities.

Basketball is not a one-player game, and LeBron knows that better than anyone. From his early days with the Cleveland Cavaliers to his championships with the Miami Heat and the triumphant return to the Cavaliers, LeBron has shown everyone that success in basketball was all about working together with teammates.

Imagine playing an instrument for your school's band. It's important to work together and sound as one. If one instrument is not working with the team, the entire sound of the music won't sound right. Basketball is a bit like that. LeBron will often make the right pass to a teammate or know the right things to say. He always wants his teammates to do well because he knows that means the entire team could do well. Because of this, many legendary players, including Dwyane Wade, Chris Bosh, and Anthony Davis, wanted to play with LeBron.

LeBron doesn't just shine on the court; he is also a superstar in making a positive impact where it matters most—in his community. LeBron founded the LeBron James Family Foundation, like his big club, an organization that wants to give back to people who are not as safe or happy as him. He wants to use it to make the world a little bit happier and help give other people the chance to succeed that he was given.

LeBron also opened the "I PROMISE School" in his hometown of Akron, Ohio. It's not just a regular school; it's a place where unfortunate and unlucky kids get the support they need to succeed. The program has been really successful. It's like making a promise to be a superhero to kids who need it most. He continues to help them with school and dreams and cheers them on just like your family cheers for you. LeBron's commitment to education shows us that being a community hero is not just about scoring points but about making sure everyone gets a fair shot at winning in life.

He showed us that, whether on the basketball court or in our communities, everything is about more than individual success. It's about lifting each other up, being a leader when needed, and using our strengths and good fortunes to make the world a better place.

Imagine you have a big box of snacks—too many snacks for just yourself. Instead of keeping them all for yourself, you decide to share them with your hungry friends. Just like when you share your snacks with friends to make them happy and fed, LeBron shares his time, money, and love with his community. He's like a superhero, using his powers to make the world better and happier.

If you look closely, these are the qualities of a good leader. LeBron isn't just a basketball player; he's also a fantastic leader. Think about when you play your favorite game with friends. A leader is someone who helps the team work together and complete their goals. Being a leader is like being the captain of your rocket ship or the queen of your castle. It can be like having a map that guides everyone to success or helping your team find the map. Whether passing the ball to a teammate or helping his friends in the community, LeBron shows us that being a leader means caring for others and making sure everyone feels like part of the team. This is why LeBron's teams have won so many championships.

Look how he's embraced the responsibility of being a role model for kids all around the world. LeBron shows that hard work and determination can help you achieve your dreams, no matter where you come from.

Let's use this as inspiration to follow his example. Look for ways to be a better leader and team player for your friends and family. Being a leader means helping others be their best, guiding and encouraging them. It could be showing others how to do better on the next math test or the best way to beat that video game. Being a team player means knowing how to do your part to help and even letting other people be the leader sometimes. Even at home, being a team player means helping out with chores, setting the table, and helping make family time super fun. You can do your part as a leader and team player in anything you do!

When you are winning, doing well, and happy, remember to give back to others. That's something LeBron did well at. He was so successful, but he remembered to give back to others and his community. He did not come from an easy background, so he knows there are others out there who can be helped.

So, aim to be like LeBron James—helping others, making a difference, and being the best team player ever. Whether it's playing basketball, acing school projects, or just being a good son, daughter, sibling, or friend.

ACTIVITY

Take some time to answer these questions, and invite an adult to help you.

- Let's remember when you had to work as part of a team. What role did you play, and what was the outcome?

- What kind of leadership qualities do you have or want to build?
- Identify a cause or issue you care about in your family, school, neighborhood, or community. Brainstorm ways you can contribute or make a difference, even in a small way.

CHAPTER FIVE

STEPHEN CURRY: FROM UNDERDOG TO THE GREATEST SHOOTER EVER

"Make it work no matter what you have to work with—that's something that stuck with me very early on as a point guard. Adjust. Get creative. Try a different angle, a different lane, a different move, or a different shot—just make it work."

—STEPHEN CURRY

Very few would have predicted that a small, skinny kid would go on to completely change the game of basketball and become known as the greatest shooter to ever play the game. There was so much doubt that it would have been easy to give up, but thanks to his dedication and belief in himself, he never did. Let's dive into the remarkable story of Stephen Curry.

Wardell Stephen Curry (Steph Curry) was born in Akron, Ohio, on March 14, 1988. He spent most of his childhood growing up in Charlotte, North Carolina. His father, Dell Curry, played for the Charlotte Hornets for most of his career. Dell was a pretty good shooter, and it was through him that Steph learned the fundamentals of basketball by watching and practicing with his dad.

Although his father was a professional athlete, his mom, Sonya, was also a former Division 1 college volleyball player. She was the one who truly taught him the discipline of training while his father was away on road trips for his NBA games. Discipline means training yourself to do something all the time so that it becomes a habit. It means doing that thing when it is time to do it, no matter how you feel or what else you want to do. Steph constantly credits his mom with shaping who he became mentally and emotionally.

After his father retired, Steph transferred to Charlotte Christian School, where he was named All-Conference and All-State. He led his team to three conference titles and three state playoff appearances, finishing his senior year shooting 48 percent from three-point range.

Both Steph's parents were college athletes at Virginia Tech, so naturally, Steph wanted to play for the Virginia Tech Hokies just like his parents. The problem, however, was that Steph was a tiny and slender player, weighing only 160 pounds. He was considered small for a basketball player, especially a guard. Even though he had achieved success on the court in high school, college scouts were worried that his size and skill would not be enough to compete at the college level. This resulted in Virginia Tech only offering him a walk-on spot, where he would receive no playing time and no scholarship to attend the school.

No matter how much you achieve, there will always be people who doubt and overlook you, but you only need one person to give you a chance. One person to believe in your skills and abilities, and for Steph, that person was Davidson College head coach Bobby McKillop. Davidson College was a small liberal arts college in North Carolina that saw something special in Stephen. Coach McKillop recognized his skills not only as a shooter but also as a leader who could take charge of the court and lead his team to victory. They offered him a scholarship, and after much consideration, he finally accepted.

In his second game with Davidson College, he scored thirty-two points against the University of Michigan. He earned the Southern Conference Freshman of the Year with honors. In his second season, he carried the Wildcats to a spot in the regional finals of the NCAA with a series of high-scoring performances. This made him a national star. In his third and final season, he led the nation with an average of 28.6 points per game as a college junior, shattering all-time records at Davidson College. At this point, he decided to join the NBA draft, where the Golden State Warriors selected him as the seventh pick.

Even at this point of getting drafted, size was still a concern. While Steph lacked size, he would make up for it double time with his skills.

Even though he was smaller than the typical NBA player, he proved that size doesn't always matter. He would have a strong finish to his rookie year, averaging twenty-two points after the 2010 All-Star Game and finishing second in the Rookie of the Year voting. This earned him a spot on the US men's basketball team, which won the gold medal in the 2010 World Championships.

Over the next few years, Stephen would face challenges with frequent ankle injuries, miss most games, and raise concerns about his body's strength to keep up with the NBA level of play. People doubted he could become a superstar and lead his team to championships. However, Steph would overcome these injuries and make a comeback in the 2012–13 season, setting an NBA record of 272 three-pointers in a single season. He would lead the Warriors to an upset against the Denver Nuggets in the first round of the playoffs, a team that nobody expected them to beat.

Steph Curry and the Warriors would continue to take the league by storm, using a style of play that involved heavy three-point shooting and teamwork. This was the first time anyone had seen a team play like that. Steph went on to win his first NBA MVP award in the regular season. Then, they defeated the team led by the great LeBron James and won the 2015 NBA Championship, beginning their dynasty.

The Warriors would dominate the next season and have a record-breaking 73–9 regular season record, beating Michael Jordan's Chicago Bulls record of 72–10. Steph Curry became the first person to win NBA MVP with a unanimous vote, meaning nobody voted against him that year. Unfortunately, the season would end in defeat, losing the 2016 NBA Championship to LeBron James. Steph and the Warriors would keep on going, and by signing their new star teammate, Kevin Durant, they would win back-to-back championships in 2017 and 2018.

Steph's incredible shooting ability has completely revolutionized the game of basketball. He is universally recognized as the best shooter in NBA history. He takes difficult three-point shots and constantly sinks them into the basket, even if the opponent is guarding him closely. Every year, he continues to break new records. In the 2021–22 NBA season, Steph passed Ray Allen and became the player with the most all-time three-pointers made in NBA history, marking himself as the king of three-point shooting. Later that year, Steph and the Warriors would win their fourth NBA Championship and his first NBA Finals MVP. Because of how much success Steph and the Warriors had, the entire NBA has now followed their style of shooting a lot of three-pointers.

"I never really set out to change the game. I never thought that would happen in my career," Steph said after receiving the MVP honor. "What I wanted to do was just be myself... I know it inspires a lot of the next generation, a lot of people who love the game of basketball, to value the skill of it, value the fact that you can work every single day to get better. You've got to be able to put in the time and the work. That's how I got here; that's how I continue to get better every single day."

As of today, Steph has won four NBA Championships, two MVPs, and a Finals MVP. He was also an NBA All-Star ten times and an All-Star MVP. He has set numerous records both in the NCAA and the NBA, especially in three-point shooting, and is one of the most celebrated basketball players in the NBA.

No matter how he or his team might be performing, Steph attracts the attention of fans around the world. He plays with a contagious joy and does things on the basketball court that nobody else can do, like regularly making half-court shots. Being a small and skinny kid didn't mean he couldn't leave his own unique impact on the game.

LESSONS FROM STEPHEN CURRY

Steph's story perfectly shows how believing in yourself, and not being discouraged by the people who doubt you, can lead to success. Steph was not a highly scouted player; very few schools were interested in recruiting him for their basketball program, even though his dad was an NBA player. He went to a small college that wasn't known for its basketball program. Still, he used this opportunity to improve his skills, especially his shooting and dribbling skills.

He could have decided to quit since no one saw potential in him. He could have given up on his dream and settled for a different life, but he didn't. He used that small stage he had been given to show the world his skills and dedication to the game. He was not afraid to face opponents bigger than him, and his commitment and discipline in training and improving himself placed him in the limelight so he could be drafted by the Golden State Warriors.

Even after he became an NBA Champion, he got injured. Many athletes quit playing the game after an injury, but Steph did the opposite. He went to therapy, put in the time and work, and returned stronger and better. He led the league in scoring and broke the record for most three-pointers in the NBA's history.

How do you think everyone who doubted and passed him over felt when they saw him rise to fame like a volcanic eruption? He never allowed other people's opinions of him to pull him down and instead kept his eyes on his goal. Never let anyone tell you that you cannot do something. If you have decided to achieve something, keep your eyes on your desired result and work toward it.

Steph could have gone to college and been an average player since he was in an average college. However, he chose a different path. He spent his time not feeling sorry for himself but practicing his skills. He practiced consistently for many hours every day so he could become the best shooter in NBA history. It is not enough to have a goal; you must be ready and willing to put in the effort it takes to master the skills necessary to achieve your dreams.

We can emulate some of Steph's behaviors to help us achieve our goals and become great people. The first of these is self-confidence. This means you trust yourself, your abilities, and your work ethic. You have faith in your ability to complete specific tasks. Steph had confidence in himself even when others didn't. He knew he had what it took to succeed as a basketball player. His trust in his abilities kept him going, even when it seemed like he was doomed to fail. Even if he played poorly, Steph trusted that if he practiced for enough hours, he would eventually play well. You can boost your self-confidence by putting in the effort and practice. You can boost your self-confidence by being friends with people who make you feel good about yourself. Avoid people who don't want the best for you or don't encourage you. Don't compare yourself to others. Everyone is on their own journey.

Another thing Steph shows us is humility. Understand that you are not perfect. You might be great at one thing, but you might also be the worst at another. Understand that you have much to be grateful for and can't succeed by yourself. Steph understood this and stayed humble. He never tried to lift himself above others or put them down for not being as good as him on the court. Despite being a massive star in the NBA, he was willing to be the second option to Kevin Durant if it meant the team would succeed. That's true humility.

Finally, perseverance. This means never giving up. This means continuing to do something even though you are still waiting to see the results. Steph was a good basketball player in high school. He practiced and trained constantly but was not chosen by the colleges he wanted to attend. Did he give up? No. He went to another school and continued to work toward his dreams. Even if you don't achieve your goal on the first try, don't give up!!

Doubts and criticisms are a part of the process of achieving your dreams. Instead of running away from the challenges, embrace them! Steph was considered too small and too weak to be an NBA player. But he refused to let this stop him. Instead, he used this as motivation to get better and improve his skills. Use others' criticisms as fuel to drive you. Never let them keep you down.

Another thing you can do is focus on your strengths. Steph was an amazing shooter. That was what he was good at and what he did. Play to your strengths and watch yourself soar to incredible heights.

ACTIVITY

Take some time to answer these questions, and invite an adult to help you.

- Can you think of a time when you were underestimated? How did you respond, and what did you learn from that experience?
- Think of role models you admire or who are great at what they do. Would you say they are humble, similar to how Steph Curry is humble?
- Do you find joy and show it off while doing your hobbies and passions?
- Identify a skill or area you want to improve. Set a goal for yourself and outline a practice routine, taking inspiration from Steph's dedication to his craft.

CHAPTER SIX

DIANA TAURASI: THE ALL-TIME LEADING SCORER OF THE WNBA

"Success is not measured by how many times you fall, but by how many times you get back up."

—DIANA TAURASI

Michael Jordan and LeBron James show us amazing examples of men who became amazing basketball legends in the NBA. But just like the NBA for men, there's also the WNBA for women. That's right—girls and women can play basketball, too. Women can be amazing basketball players. One lady is an absolute scoring legend in the WNBA, and she never let the fact that she was a girl stop her from following her dreams. That player is Diana Taurasi.

Diana Taurasi showed that girls can achieve anything. The saying, "Don't let anyone tell you that you can't do something, especially because you're a girl," perfectly fits her story. Let's explore how she loved basketball, broke stereotypes, and became a role model for girls who dream big in sports.

In the quiet streets of Chino, California, the rhythmic bounce of a basketball echoed through Diana Taurasi's early years. Diana was born on June 11, 1982, in Glendale, California, to a family that embraced sports. Her father was a professional soccer player in Italy, so he introduced Diana to soccer and basketball. She would practice both, but in high school, she decided to focus entirely on basketball.

Her family played a pivotal role in fueling her passion. From her first dribbles in the driveway to organized games, Diana's parents and siblings encouraged her. They taught her that being a girl didn't limit her potential. Their loving support created a healthy environment where she could thrive and dream big.

As a young girl, Diana's basketball journey had its challenges. There are often stereotypes in the world saying girls can't play sports as well as guys can. Because guys are usually taller and more muscular than girls, girls shouldn't even play. This led to sports being played by mostly boys during this time. Girls are often pushed to do other things like cheerleading, arts, and academics. What helped Diana was her family, who became her greatest advocates. Their mantra, "Don't let anyone tell you that you can't do something, especially because you're a girl," became the guiding light of her early career.

Diana found her happy place in the community courts and school gyms. She worked on her skills in these spaces, driven by a deep love for the game and the desire to prove that her gender should never be a barrier to success. Her early experiences laid the foundation for a strong spirit that would carry her through the highs and lows of her future in basketball.

Before her college career, Diana had a challenging time dealing with her parents' divorce during her teenage years. Despite the tough times, she used basketball to escape, focusing on the sport to get through them. This likely helped her become resilient and mentally strong as she pursued her basketball journey. Despite all of this, Diana would have an amazing high school career.

She enrolled at the University of Connecticut to play basketball, where her skills truly blossomed. As a "UConn Husky," she led her team to three consecutive championships, showcasing her skills and determination on the court. Her success in college laid the foundation for a legendary professional career. Because of her college success, the Phoenix Mercury selected her as the first overall pick in the WNBA in 2004.

Diana's impact was immediate, earning her Rookie of the Year honors and marking the beginning of her ascent to WNBA stardom. The Phoenix Mercury became Diana's stage for breaking records and setting new standards in women's basketball. Diana's ability to shoot from anywhere on the court and her knack for making crucial plays in clutch moments made her a force to be reckoned with. When teams would play against Diana, they would be worried about her ability to score so many points, no matter what they did to defend against her. Her leadership skills and competitive spirit brought success to her team and inspired a generation of young basketball lovers.

Diana currently has three WNBA Championships, is a WNBA Finals MVP, has several All-Star appearances, and is now the all-time leading scorer in WNBA history. Nobody has scored more points in the WNBA than Diana, and she still scores more and more points every year, making her record even harder to beat.

There was no way Diana was going to believe that only boys and men could be truly successful in sports. She dribbled past those old ideas and took her shots to prove that girls can be basketball legends, too. That is how resilient and competitive she is.

Diana's amazing skills and determination inspired a new generation of girls who love sports. When you see girls playing basketball or soccer, you can think of Diana Taurasi and how she helped make it possible. So, remember, whether you're into basketball, soccer, or any sport, you can dream big and go for it.

LESSONS FROM DIANA TAURASI

Similar to looking at Michael Jordan and LeBron James, Diana wasn't just handed her skills and success. She didn't wake up one day magically being awesome; she worked really hard for it. Diana showed us that dedication and hard work are the secrets to being excellent at what you love. Never forget that you can't just magically wake up great at something. It takes practice and work.

She showed us that it's not about being perfect from the start. The most important thing is that you just get started. If you love what you do, practicing and training is much easier and more fun. You shouldn't feel like you are forcing yourself to practice. Of course, practice is not always the most fun thing to do, but your desire to become better should excite you to practice. She practiced and practiced, never forgetting that this was a game she loved dearly. Even when she would always hear about how basketball is meant for boys, that never stopped her

Imagine finding something you are so excited to do, and it feels like time flies by—those might be clues that something is your passion. For Diana Taurasi, her passion was basketball; just like her, you can discover and chase your passions. Whether it's drawing, singing, or playing with robots, take some time to explore what makes you feel super excited. Let that passion be your guide when you find it, like Diana with her basketball. Your passions are like treasure maps leading to a world of fun and fulfillment.

Even when it was tough, she never gave up. That's what we call dedication. When you are passionate and enjoy doing something so much, you have a better chance of not giving up when things don't go your way or when they get really hard. So, whether you're into drawing, dancing, or playing an instrument, if you stay dedicated and keep trying, you too can be excellent despite what anybody might tell you.

When we look at Diana's story, she might have seemed so natural on the court, as if it had always been smooth sailing for her. But the truth is it wasn't. She faced challenges and setbacks, just like we do in our own lives. But did she let those tough times bring her down? No way. Diana taught us the power of resilience—bouncing back when things get tough. When her parents got divorced, she didn't forget about her dreams. She used basketball as a way to make herself feel happier.

So, channel your inner Diana the next time you find yourself dealing with a tricky situation or facing a tough problem. Take a deep breath, remind yourself you're strong, and tackle it with determination. Spend time doing things that you enjoy and make you happy. Resilience is like your superhero shield, protecting you as you face the ups and downs of life. Lean on the people who are important to you and can help you keep going. If there are people who love you and support your dreams, cherish them forever.

Diana Taurasi's qualities are like a playbook for being your own kind of hero. Being resilient means facing challenges with courage, and having a passion for what you do is like having your own superpower. So, let Diana inspire you to explore different things until you find your own magic.

Being a girl doesn't stop you from being a sports superstar. Neither does being a certain color or shape. Neither does coming from a certain background or family. If you're passionate about something, like Diana is about basketball, you can become a legend too. Aim high, score high. Grab your basketballs, soccer balls, robots, musical instruments, or whatever you love, and go out there—the world is your court.

ACTIVITY

Take some time to answer these questions, and invite an adult to help you.

- Do you feel like you aren't fit to do something you love? Like how girls weren't expected to play basketball? How can you overcome that feeling?
- Think about something difficult that has happened to you. What did you do to help you be resilient?
- Who are your greatest supporters, and what can you do to show them that you appreciate them?

CHAPTER SEVEN

SUE BIRD: A CAREER OF CONSISTENCY AND CHAMPIONSHIPS

"Whether I retire tomorrow or in twenty years, I want to get as much out as possible."

—SUE BIRD

There is only one basketball player ever, male or female, to have won five Olympic gold medals, four Women's National Basketball Association (WNBA) Championships, and four EuroLeague titles. She is recognized worldwide as the greatest player in the WNBA and a basketball legend. In this chapter, we will look at who she is and how he came to have such a long-lasting and incredible career with the WNBA.

Suzanne Brigit Bird was born on October 6, 1980, in Syosset, New York, to Herschel and Nancy Bird. She has an elder sister, Jen, who inspired her love of basketball, soccer, tennis, and track and field. Sue said that she wanted to do whatever her sister did and that she was fortunate that her sister decided to pick up a basketball.

At eleven years old, in the sixth grade, Sue began playing in the Amateurs Athletic Union basketball game. She continued to play basketball in her first and second years at Syosset High School. After transferring to Christ the King Regional High School in Queens for her third and fourth years, the Royals had an undefeated season in Sue's third year. They won the New York State Championship and the National title in her senior year. She also played in the Women's Basketball Coaches Association High School All-America game and scored eleven points.

Several colleges, including the University of Connecticut, Stanford University, and Vanderbilt University, actively scouted her. She decided to enroll at the University of Connecticut (UConn), where she joined the women's basketball team.

Her coach called her aside once and told her that anything that happens in the game is her fault. This confused Sue since she knew basketball was played as a team. Still, she finally understood that her coach was asking her to take on responsibility for her team, the game, and herself. She was being asked to be a leader and guide for the team. At the time, she was shy and reserved, but hearing her coach say that, she did what she could to break out of her shell.

As a leader, she understood that her team's results would be driven by how much responsibility she was able and willing to take. It did not matter if they were working as a team; she must be able to drive her team members to a common goal. Sue came to understand this because of that conversation with her coach.

She knew that she needed to become a more vocal leader. A leader who spoke up and that the team could look up to. To achieve this, she had to change everyone's views about her. They had come to know her as this shy and reserved person, but she could change that. If she began to be more vocal and confident, people would start to see this new side of her over time.

As a result of this shift in her mindset to become a great leader, she led her team to a 36–1 record at the Big East Championship and the 2000 NCAA Women's Division 1 Basketball Tournament. While in her junior season, the Huskies went 32–3 with the final loss against UConn's Big East rival Notre Dame in the Final Four Tournament. In her final season, the Huskies went 39–0, and Sue won the Wade Trophy, Honda Sports Award, and Naismith Award as College Player of the Year.

As Sue's basketball days ended at UConn, she set several records. She won awards that honored her performances in scoring, assists, steals, three-point percentage, and free-throw percentage. She also won two National Championships, three Big East Championships, and regular season titles. She was the inaugural winner of the Nancy Lieberman Award in 2000, 2001, and 2002.

Sue said that the moment she finished her final season at the University of Connecticut, it was a whirlwind period until she got drafted by the WNBA. Sue was selected by the Seattle Storm as the first overall pick of the 2002 WNBA draft. In her first season, the Storm had a 17–15 record and lost in the playoffs. Sue was not used to losing and had to change her point of view about it. She had to accept that she needed to be patient and accept losing as part of learning and growth.

Sue also experienced some difficulties in working with Lauren Jackson, who was also the first overall pick by the Seattle Storm the previous year. Jackson was not a fan of Sue; she felt she was overhyped and not as good as people said. However, they had amazing chemistry on the court. Sue said she had to gain Jackson's trust and respect by closely listening to what she had to say during the games. By working to earn the respect and trust of her team-mates, Sue ensured that their team had good synergy and worked like a well-oiled machine. As a leader, Sue knew that sometimes you have to listen more than you speak.

In the summer of 2004, Sue played in her first Olympics. She was intimidated at first by the other team members, which included some of the best in the game, including Dawn Staley and Lisa Leslie. She was worried about being a vocal leader when she did not have as much experience as these women. She watched them make their decisions and tried to understand the reason for each decision they made. She was studying those who were more experienced and vocal than her. By doing this, she would gain more self-confidence and become a better leader.

Sometimes, you will be in a room with people with more experience than you or who have already established themselves in your chosen path. While feeling intimidated is okay, you should still contribute to the group's conversations. Take your time proving yourself. That opportunity will come. Watch and learn and determine the best way for you to contribute.

Sue was the first WNBA player in history to score at least 5000 points and 2000 assists in their career. At the time, she was the only WNBA player to have achieved this in basketball history. By age twenty-three, Sue had won more than expected. She had been selected for twelve All-Star games and been awarded an All-WNBA selection eight times.

Sue has long been an advocate for equality and social justice in women's sports. She has spoken up for the rights of the LGBTQIA+ community and stood with her African American teammates to call out for social justice. She also founded an organization committed to promoting the rights of female athletes.

LESSONS FROM SUE BIRD

Sue Bird's career has demonstrated the importance of reliability and steady progress in many ways. She has shown that she can be counted on to deliver a high-quality performance in every game and every season. She has never let any situation like injury or the opinions of others affect how she plays her game. She has played in every WNBA season since her debut in 2002 and has never missed a single international competition. She has been praised continually by everyone she works with. From coaches to teammates, everyone agrees that she is pleasant to work with and always brings her A game.

She has constantly improved her skills, showing that steady progress in adapting to new situations and overcoming challenges is possible. She is a player who can adapt to a variety of roles, such as point guard, shooting guard, captain, and mentor. She has consistently overcome injuries, age, and competition to remain at the very top of her game.

Leadership is one of the virtues we can learn from Sue. However, it might seem hard to be a leader. A good trick is to put yourself in the other person's shoes and ask yourself how you would like to be spoken to or treated if you were them. As a leader, you must identify the goal that your team is walking toward. It may be getting the other team's flag on the playground or completing a project. Once you identify the goal, give everyone tasks they can do, and make sure they are tasks they *can* do or that you can show them how to do them. A leader's goal is to unite everyone toward one goal, even if you have a group of very different people.

She adopted a leadership style that carried all her team members along. By using vocal leadership, she ensured that all members of her team were on the same page, both on and off the court.

Younger team members have also called her a fantastic mentor. She is willing to take time out of her day to explain how something works and why. She never put anyone down or made them feel like less because they did not completely understand a specific concept. This enabled her to move seamlessly into her advocacy role as she can work with individuals playing different sports, and some who are not even athletes, to achieve a common goal.

It's important to note that Sue was not a natural leader. As a young kid, she was shy and reserved, and she had to learn how to become more vocal and confident to lead her team. Even when Sue was a great player and got into the WNBA, she had to develop the confidence to lead at this new level. She did this by closely studying and listening to other team leaders. Remember to stay humble and know that there is always something you can learn or improve.

We can emulate Sue's persistence and perseverance in chasing her goals. Develop a "can't stop, won't stop" attitude. Regardless of the challenges that you face and any obstacles in your path, it would be best if you remained determined to your end result. There is nothing like an easy path or an easily achievable goal. Understand that anything worth having requires hard work and sacrifice.

You must also use your voice and platform to help other people. It could be as simple as speaking up for the unpopular kid getting bullied at school or supporting those who do not have as much as you. Be an advocate for equality and change. Treat everyone how they deserve to be treated, and if you have been treating someone poorly, you still have an opportunity to change and treat them with respect.

Consistency is very important in life, but it can take a lot of work to build a habit of doing things consistently. It helps to start small. For example, if your goal is to get better at the cello, you may need to practice for two hours a day to become a master. Practicing for two hours from the beginning may be difficult. You can start by practicing for ten minutes, then twenty, then thirty minutes. Eventually, you will be able to practice for an hour, and if you keep building on that, you will be able to practice for two hours and get better. Remember, small, consistent growth is better than making a giant leap once in a while.

Remember that you are the only one who makes decisions about your future. Where you end up in life is completely up to you. Determine what you want to do and work toward it. Sue Bird is an amazing player and leader, but that didn't come naturally. She had to put in the work to get there, and you can do the same, too.

ACTIVITY

Take some time to answer these questions, and invite an adult to help you.

- Think of an area in your life where you can be more consistent. How can this consistency help you achieve your goals?
- Do you consider yourself a natural leader? If so, what are your leadership qualities? If not, what can you do to become a better leader?
- Identify a cause or issue you are passionate about. As inspired by Sue Bird's advocacy work, plan a small project or action to help this cause.

ALL-TIME GREATEST BASKETBALL STORIES FOR KIDS

15 LEGENDARY HOOPS JOURNEYS, LIFE LESSONS, AND HEROIC ATHLETES TO INSPIRE YOUNG READERS TO OVERCOME CHALLENGES AND FOLLOW THEIR DREAMS

Hey there, young hoopers!

You know how exciting it is when you make a great pass and it helps your team score? Well, I've got a special request that's kind of like making that great assist—you might not score, but you'll help someone else do it!

Our goal is to inspire kids everywhere with stories of challenge and triumph on the basketball court. Every shot, game, and season has a lesson behind it, and I want to share these lessons with as many kids as possible.

But I need your help to do it. A lot of people decide which books to read based on reviews. So, I'm asking you to help other kids discover these amazing stories by asking your parents, teacher or coach to leave a review for this book.

Think of it like this: your review could help...

- another kid learn how to deal with a tough loss.
- a friend find the courage to try out for the basketball team.
- someone your age get inspired to follow their dream, just like their favorite player.

And the best part? It doesn't cost a dime and takes less than a minute! Just scan the QR code below to leave your review:

If you're the kind of person who likes helping others, then you're already part of the team. Welcome aboard! I can't wait to show you all the cool plays, moves, and strategies you'll read about in the next chapters.

Thanks a million for your help. You're not just a reader; you're a game-changer.

PS - Remember, sharing something valuable with someone makes you a key player in their eyes. If you think this book can help another kid, why not pass it along? Just like a good pass, it could lead to a great bucket.

CHAPTER EIGHT

LISA LESLIE: BREAKING BARRIERS IN WOMEN'S BASKETBALL

"No matter what accomplishments you make, somebody helped you."

—LISA LESLIE

L isa Leslie is a former basketball player who has won many awards and accolades for her awesome gameplay and leadership abilities. She is recognized as one of the greatest female basketball players ever and helped make professional women's basketball a reality. Before becoming the awesome basketball player, coach, and role model she is today—she was a kid just like you. Let's look at Lisa's life and journey to become one of the most iconic basketball players in the WNBA.

Lisa DeShaun Leslie was born on July 7, 1972, in Gardena, California, and raised by her mother, Christine Leslie Espinoza. Lisa grew up in Compton with her mother, who worked as a mail carrier and a truck driver, often having to be away from home for work. While her mother was away, Lisa lived with some of her relatives and babysat her younger sister, Tiffany. Lisa had to be strong as a young girl to be away from her mother and help care for her sister.

When she was twelve years old, Lisa was already six feet tall. For a twelve-year-old girl, this is pretty tall. Because she was so tall, everyone assumed she would play basketball. Still, Lisa only played basketball once she got to junior high. A classmate invited her to try out for the team. Lisa was a very shy kid, so she went to the tryout to see if this was a way for her to make some friends. A tryout is when different people compete against each other for a position on a team.

During the tryout, the coach divided the players into two teams—a team of people who used their left hand (left-handed team) and a team of players who used their right hand (right-handed team). Leslie was the only left-handed player in the group. She did not like being alone like that, so she promised herself she would learn how to play with her right hand. This decision led her to become ambidextrous, meaning she could play with either hand she wanted with equal ability, a fantastic skill for a basketball player.

Leslie's cousin and her uncle taught her how to play, teaching her the fundamentals and encouraging her to play a more physical type of basketball. When Leslie was in the eighth grade, she joined a boy's team. At first, the boys refused to give her the ball, but in one of the games, Lisa stole a pass between two of her teammates and scored a point. After that, they shouted, "Give the ball to the girl!!" Even though the boys weren't helping her at first, she decided to take action into her own hands.

Lisa continued to develop her skills, and soon enough, she started playing in the Olympic Girls' Development League, often against girls who were way older than her. The OGDL helped Lisa meet many college coaches, and she received over a hundred recruitment offers before she even entered high school.

Lisa went to Morningside High School and was named California's "Freshman of the Year" after her first high school basketball season. The team made it to the State Championship game in her second year (1987–88). Lisa played an excellent game but missed the final shot because time ran out, and Morningside lost by one point to Fremont High School. The crushing defeat made Lisa determined to lead her team to the championship the following year. She did that when they defeated Fremont in a State Championship rematch in 1989. *USA Today* and *Parade* magazine named Lisa to their first-team high school All-America squads that year.

When she was sixteen, Lisa joined the American junior national team and traveled out of the country for the first time. Even though she was the only high school student on the team, Lisa led the team in scoring and rebounding throughout the tournament. As a high school senior, Lisa scored an unbelievable 101 points in the first half, setting a national record and leading her team to their second consecutive State Championship. She also won the Naismith Award given to the nation's top high school basketball player.

Lisa then attended the University of Southern California (USC). As a college basketball player, she led the team to an 89–31 overall record and four consecutive NCAA Tournament appearances. This means the team won eighty-nine games and only lost thirty-one games during her time with them, and their gameplay was so excellent that they qualified for the tournament four times. She was named the 1991 National Freshman of the Year and the 1994 Naismith College Player of the Year. Lisa also received All-American honors in 1992, 1993, and 1994. Lisa set Pac-10 conference records for scoring, rebounding, and blocked shots and became the first player to make the first All-Conference team in each of her four years. Lisa graduated from USC with a bachelor's degree in communications.

At that time, there were no opportunities for women to be professional basketball players in the US. So, like many other college stars, Lisa signed with a team in the European women's professional league. She joined Sicilgesso, based in Italy, for the 1994–95 season. Lisa then made the 1996 US Olympic team and helped lead the team to a gold medal. While doing this, she set a record when she scored thirty-five points in one game.

After the Olympics, Lisa was unsure if she wanted to keep playing overseas, so she looked to other careers back in the US. Fortunately, however, the WNBA was established in the summer of 1997, so Lisa, along with Sheryl Swoopes and Rebecca Lobo, became the faces and first members of the new league. Lisa anchored her hometown team, the Los Angeles Sparks.

Lisa played in the WNBA for twelve seasons, leading the Sparks to League Championships in 2001 and 2002. She was a seven-time All-Star (and three-time All-Star Game MVP), three-time WNBA MVP, eight-time first-team All-WNBA honoree, and two-time Defensive Player of the Year. Lisa made history when she became the first player in the WNBA to dunk on July 30, 2002. This event was groundbreaking because it showed the world her skill and talent and inspired future generations of female basketball players and sportswomen.

Off the court, Lisa was recognized by the Big Sisters Guild of Los Angeles for her work with foster children. She earned her master's degree in business administration from the University of Phoenix. In 2005, Lisa married Michael Lockwood, a commercial pilot. They have two children, Lauren and Michael II.

Lisa continued to bring home victories with Team USA during these years. In addition to FIBA World Championship titles in 1998 and 2002, the US women's basketball team won gold in the Olympics in 2000, 2004, and 2008, making Lisa a four-time gold medalist. In 2019, Lisa was selected for the US Olympic & Paralympic Hall of Fame.

LESSONS FROM LISA LESLIE

Lisa Leslie was more than a basketball player. Her grace, skill, and leadership abilities made her a beacon of hope and inspiration to young girls all over the world who dreamed of a basketball career. She was an example to a whole generation of female athletes, showing them they could excel at the highest levels of their chosen sport. In 2015, she was inducted into the Naismith Memorial Basketball Hall of Fame and the Women's Basketball Hall of Fame. Her journey is a strong example of resilience, consistent excellence, and the power of breaking barriers.

Lisa was one of the first advocates for equality in sports. She championed the cause of women's sports, using her platform to speak for female athletes. Lisa pushed for equal treatment of athletes and disrupted several stereotypes. She became a voice that the younger generation looked up to for hope and direction. She set a high standard of excellence and challenged other female athletes to reach for greater heights and not settle for less. She helped kick off professional women's basketball in the US and increased the WNBA's popularity. People traveled from far and near to watch her play and became exposed to the excellence of the league.

After her retirement, she now serves as the head coach of the triplets in the BIG3 Professional Basketball League. She also offers insight as a commentator and studio analyst for Orlando Magic broadcasts, increasing viewers' understanding and enriching their experience.

Lisa's skills on the court challenged stereotypes about the physical abilities of women. She proved that women can be just as good in sports and provided more visibility to women's sports. Popular basketball players at the time were mostly male. As a black woman, Lisa symbolized that excellence does not know racial or gender boundaries. She also broke social barriers by becoming a role model and a voice for other female athletes. She encouraged other female athletes to speak up about their talents and skills. She broke gender barriers and racial barriers just by being her awesome self.

Lisa was determined to achieve her dreams. When there was no platform for her to pursue basketball professionally in the US, she went to Europe to chase her dreams. She never let anything or anyone stop her. She was a pioneer of female professional basketball in the US. She faced several challenges but stayed true to her purpose and eventually succeeded. In whatever you want to do, never give up. You may be the first person to do something, and others may try to discourage you and tell you it won't work out for you. Still, if you are determined, you will eventually achieve your dreams.

While determination is a great trait to have, on its own, it does not guarantee success. You need to also develop the necessary skills to accompany it. A very important skill needed to achieve your dream is leadership skills. A leader has the courage to face challenges and bring others with them. A leader can provide support to others and not put others down. Lisa was a leader. Even when she succeeded, she pulled other female athletes with her. She showed values like humility, positive thinking, resilience, and hard work.

One way to cultivate and demonstrate leadership skills is in advocacy. Advocacy is speaking up for someone who cannot speak up for themselves. If a classmate is being bullied, speak up for them.

Stand up to the bullies on their behalf. You may not be praised for it, but you will have done the right thing, and in the end, that is what matters. You must be able to challenge any unfair treatment you observe. If someone is being mean to someone else because they are a boy or a girl or black or brown or white, you should tell the person that what they are doing is wrong. This is advocacy.

Dare to break barriers!! It doesn't matter where you are or what you want to do. If anything is stopping you from achieving your dreams, challenge it. Never be afraid to challenge the status quo.

ACTIVITY

Take some time to answer these questions, and invite an adult to help you.

- Think of a time when you achieved something you thought you couldn't. What did you learn from that experience?
- Talk about a girl or woman—whether a basketball player or not—who inspires you and why. She could be a teacher, coach, friend, classmate, etc.

CHAPTER NINE

GIANNIS ANTETOKOUNMPO: FROM HARDSHIP IN ATHENS TO NBA GLORY

"I am my father's legacy."

—GIANNIS ANTETOKOUNMPO

L et's learn about the great Giannis, a basketball player for the Milwaukee Bucks. He is also known as the Greek Freak because he is super fast, strong, athletic, and does really amazing things on the court. Giannis started playing basketball when he was just thirteen years old, and even though he faced many challenges, he never gave up and is now very successful. He is an NBA MVP and NBA Finals MVP, but he went through some real hardships and tough times along the way. In this chapter, we will look at Giannis' life story and how he overcame challenges to become one of the greatest players in the NBA.

In 1991, Charles and Veronica Antetokounmpo moved to Greece from Nigeria in search of better opportunities and a better life for their family. On December 6, 1994, they had a son whom they named Giannis, a Hebrew name meaning God's Grace. Charles and Veronica had no legal status in Greece, which means they did not have access to special advantages that citizens and legal immigrants had. Because of this, Giannis and his brother experienced discrimination and lived with the fear of deportation. Discrimination is when people treat someone else poorly because they are different from them, which is very wrong. Deportation is when someone is arrested by the police in the country where they are living and sent back to their own country In this case, Giannis and his family would have been sent back to Nigeria.

Giannis and his family lived in poverty and struggled to make ends meet, so he and his brothers had to sell small items such as bags, sunglasses, and other things on the streets of Athens to feed themselves and contribute to the family's finances. Sometimes, they would need to run away from the police, who would try to arrest them for selling items. It was a tough life, but they worked together as a family to make things work.

At first, Giannis and his brothers only played soccer (or European football), which is a very popular sport in Greece. However, in 2007, when Giannis was thirteen years old, a basketball coach called Spiros Velliniatis saw him play and noted his extraordinary physical potential. The coach saw that Giannis was faster and stronger and worked harder than others on the court. He knew that Giannis could become a much better player with some training.

Giannis' mother initially opposed him and his brother pursuing basketball because they risked being deported. Still, after the coach explained to her that basketball could offer them new opportunities and bring them success, she eventually agreed to let Giannis and his brother Thanasis play. They made a lot of progress quickly and eventually started playing for the Greece second-division team, Filathlitikos.

Eventually, almost by chance, an NBA scout would stumble upon a video of Giannis playing and become very interested in him. Soon, many scouts and agents were interested in Giannis. In 2013, eighteen-year-old Giannis entered the NBA draft with very low expectations. He was relatively unknown in the American basketball industry. However, the Milwaukee Bucks were intrigued by his raw talent. They saw the same thing coach Spiros saw in him and decided to add him to their team. He was selected as the fifteenth overall pick and began his journey in the NBA.

Going from the streets of Athens to the shiny and fashionable world of professional basketball was very strange for Giannis. He was not used to such extravagance, but he adapted really well. Although Giannis was initially a skinny and undeveloped player, he continued to work really hard to develop both his body and skills. Over time, Giannis would develop into a monstrous and powerful force on the basketball court, becoming known for his ability to use his strength and athleticism to dunk on any player in the NBA.

At the age of twenty-one, he recorded his first triple-double. A triple-double is when a player scores ten or more in three different categories. These categories include points, steals, rebounds, assists, and blocked shots. By the next season, he was invited to the All-Star game at just twenty-two years old, and at twenty-four, he won the trophy for Most Valuable Player in the NBA. Finally, it was in 2021 that Giannis truly became a legend.

The Milwaukee Bucks would make it to the 2201 NBA Finals to face the Phoenix Suns. In a best-of-seven series, where the first team to win four games wins the whole thing, Giannis' team was losing 0–2. They would go on to win four straight games, and Giannis scored fifty points in the final game six. One spectator said that it seemed like Giannis was flying. He soared for dunks and rebounds as the entire Midwest city of Milwaukee held their breath. And for the first time in fifty years, the Milwaukee Bucks won the NBA Finals. Giannis averaged 35.2 points, 13.2 rebounds, and 5.0 assists per game during the finals. But his impact was more than stats, more than points and rebounds.

His gameplay that year was off the charts. Some other players and coaches said Giannis played each game like it might be his last. This was what made him a legend. This was what turned Giannis Antetokounmpo into the Greek Freak. He became a beacon of hope and transformation. Like Tony Stark became Iron Man by putting on the suit, Giannis Antetokounmpo became the Greek Freak by picking up a ball. He moved from poverty to winning championships and achieving glory across continents. His resilience in the face of adversity became an inspiring story that people can now learn from.

There is a message that Giannis continues to send in all his MVP speeches, and every time he is asked about his success, that message is "You too can rise." This is a message of hope and has become the anthem of the underdogs. "I, too, shall rise." It is a saying that means that regardless of my upbringing or status in society, I will also try to be the best in my field or the things that I do.

Giannis averages 23.3 points, 9.7 rebounds and 4.8 assists per game. He has been an NBA All-Star seven times and won the MVP award twice and Defensive Player of the Year once. He is also the youngest since Kawhi Leonard to be an NBA MVP twice. In addition to this, he also led the Milwaukee Bucks to win the NBA Championship for the first time in fifty years. Despite these achievements, he remains humble and always remembers where he came from.

LESSONS FROM GIANNIS ANTETOKOUNMPO

The impact of Giannis is not only felt on the basketball court. His story is one of resilience, hope, and inspiration to others. He is a symbol of defeating adversity and emerging victorious. His story makes everyone facing their own struggles believe that they, too, can overcome them, just like Giannis did. His success is not his alone; it is also the success of his community. It is your success as well. Because if Giannis can become the Greek Freak, you can become what you dream of, too. You can become the best neurosurgeon, actor, firefighter, or teacher. Whenever you feel like your dreams remain out of your reach, remember the story of the boy who never gave up, the boy who continued to soar and score regardless of his situation, and gain hope from him.

Giannis' story teaches us that adversity is not supposed to stop you from achieving your dreams but should be a stepping stone to them. Think of it like this: if you are playing a video game, you want to be able to defeat the boss but to defeat the boss, you have to fight all his little minions and win. That is why games are in levels. Each level you play brings you closer to fighting the boss, and in each level, you gain new weapons and skills that will help you in your fight with the boss. Any adversity you face today is a minion for a future boss you will face. The troubles of today are training for tomorrow. Think of adversity as a learning process, an opportunity to grow and learn new skills to help you achieve your goals. This process of turning adversity into opportunity is called resilience. Resilience is something that Giannis had, and so the next time you face a challenge, reach for your inner Greek Freak. Be determined, relentless, and unyielding. Be resilient.

Giannis was a poor kid selling trinkets to survive on the streets of Athens. But inside him lay a talent, a skill that very few people have, that turned him into a champion. If his skill had not been recognized, and he hadn't put in the effort to develop that skill, he would probably not be the Greek Freak that we all know and love today. Everybody has a unique talent. They do something better than everybody else, something that only they can do. You have a unique talent, whether it is being able to sing or dance, cook or knit, solve mathematics questions, or understand complex theories. You must identify that one thing that only you can do and develop. It is not enough to have a talent in something; you must also take steps to grow your talent by constantly training and developing yourself, just like Giannis.

Another thing we can emulate from Giannis' story is his work ethic. Giannis was not afraid to work hard. Even though he had a lot of natural ability and was very tall, he kept working on himself until he became the best in his field. More is needed than just talent. You must also be willing to put in the work to develop that talent into something people will recognize. Hard work beats talent when talent doesn't work hard.

It would be best to strive to be as resilient as Giannis. Turn your adversities into opportunities. It's okay to make mistakes and to fall. It is not okay to stay down when you fall, though. Learn from your mistakes and the mistakes of others.

Try to stay humble, even when you have achieved your goal. There is a saying that pride comes before the fall, which means that once a person becomes proud, it is only a matter of time before they fall from their high horse. Just like Giannis, you will succeed thanks to your supporters and community, so remember to pass on the glory and praise, not keep it for yourself. Instead of being satisfied when you achieve your goals, set new goals. This is called having a growth mindset. Not being satisfied with your current level and constantly reaching for more while staying true to yourself and your roots.

No matter what obstacles you face or what tries to get in the way of your dreams, keep reaching for greatness. Continue learning and developing yourself to be the best version of yourself. Like Giannis, do not let your circumstances keep you from achieving your dreams.

ACTIVITY

Take some time to answer these questions, and invite an adult to help you.

- What difficult challenges have you had to overcome in your childhood? What did you learn from them?
- Identify a unique talent or skill you possess. Create a plan to develop and use this talent to achieve a personal goal, drawing inspiration from Giannis's dedication to improving his game.

CHAPTER TEN
JEREMY LIN: THE UNLIKELY RISE AND LINSANITY ERA

"Well, I'm not here to live up to anybody's expectations, I'm here to live up to mine."

—JEREMY LIN

There is a saying that if you judge a fish by its ability to climb a tree, that fish will forever remain dumb in your eyes. Jeremy Lin's early story is very similar to this analogy. Before Jeremy Lin became a beloved player in NBA history, he was a high school student who nobody expected to make it, mainly because of his appearance.

Jeremy Lin grew up in the San Francisco Bay Area. Growing up as an Asian American kid, he had certain expectations placed on him. Expectations tossed on him by his parents, teachers, and the community at large. He was a student at Palo Alto High School and was expected to succeed as both a student and an athlete. These expectations would later carry into his higher education as he went on to attend Harvard as an athlete.

Jeremy has been very vocal about his struggles during his school years and the immense pressure he was under to do well and make everyone proud. In traditional Asian culture, there is typically a huge expectation to perform well academically, which he had to balance with his basketball dreams. He even went on to admit that these pressures got to him deeply, triggering moments of depression and much worse. It's a sentiment that many young adults can relate to.

A few years back, in a heartfelt Facebook post, Jeremy penned his feelings into words that many other students can relate to:

"My daily thought process was that every homework assignment, project, and test could be the difference—the difference between a great college and a mediocre college, the difference between success and failure, the difference between happiness and misery."

However, these pressures did not stop Jeremy from pursuing his dream and inspired him to work even harder. Being a very talented basketball player and performing well in school, Jeremy expected that a good college would offer him a scholarship. To the surprise of many people, he did not receive any scholarships to play college basketball.

Jeremy wouldn't give up. He would need to go down a different path. This led him to attend Harvard, a place where his career had the opportunity to blossom. Harvard is an Ivy League school, meaning they do not offer scholarships to athletes. However, Harvard and Brown were the two colleges that offered him a spot on their team where he would actually receive playing time. Other colleges would not promise him any playing time.

Jeremy would have an impressive college career. He would set records as a player in the Ivy League and help Harvard set records for winning games. Academics would still be very important to him, and he would graduate with a degree in Economics.

Surprisingly, even with his impeccable records and undeniable skills, Jeremy wasn't drafted by the NBA after college; he was not noticed at all. This led to feelings of frustration and self-doubt, as Jeremy had to ask himself if he was ever going to be good enough to make it to the NBA.

A big part of this was racial bias. Because Jeremy was Asian American, he was easily overlooked and never considered a future star. Most players who made it to the NBA were of other ethnicities, typically not Asian. It's never easy when you have to work twice as hard as others to prove that you're worth something and that you are more than your background. This would not stop Jeremy.

His efforts finally paid off when the Golden State Warriors signed him to a two-year contract. Although he didn't get much playing time, at least his dream of being in the NBA happened. The Warriors would eventually waive him, meaning Jeremy would have no team, and he would need to wait for another team to add him. Eventually, in 2012, the New York Knicks would add Jeremy Lin to their team, and this was where his rise really began.

Even the Knicks barely gave Jeremy any playing time initially. However, the team was struggling so badly that the coach decided to let Jeremy play. Jeremy started leading the team to victory with a seven-game winning streak, where he averaged more than twenty points and seven assists per game. He became their new starting point guard.

Like a reward from the universe for his patience and perseverance, Jeremy's rise to fame was meteoric—quick and heavy. He became a symbol of something more in the Asian American community, being one of the few of his kind in the NBA. This fame led to the world-renowned "Linsanity era" in 2013. He became a global sensation, and everyone was eager to watch him play and see what he would do next. It was a remarkable turning point in his career.

A year after joining the Knicks and continuing to play well, Jeremy suffered an injury. He had a meniscus tear which would take him out for the season, denying him the opportunity to go out in a blaze of glory. However, Jeremy's impact on the basketball world is still felt strongly to this day. Fans of the New York Knicks still look back at those short but memorable weeks with a fond smile.

Eventually, he would be traded away from the Knicks and play for several other NBA teams, never quite reaching the same "Linsanity" performances that made him famous. But that was okay. Jeremy had a ton to be proud of. He is still a beloved player in NBA history to this day and an inspiration to Asian American players around the world.

LESSONS FROM JEREMY LIN

Throughout his nine-year career, Jeremy has faced many instances of racial bias and stereotyping. He expressed that he was never just a basketball player; Jeremy was always seen first as that Asian who people were quick to reject and overlook and never for the skills he brought to the court.

Jeremy's journey was tough; he had to deal with many more challenges and disappointments than the average player. Still, he always pulled through with perseverance and grace. Jeremy faced many disappointments, sure, but one thing remained constant: He never judged himself by his ability to climb but rather by his ability to swim. He never measured his life and successes by the expectations set by those around him but by the ones he set for himself.

Another notable quote is, "There's no such thing as good luck; good luck is simply opportunity meeting preparation." Jeremy didn't know when his time would come; it started to look like it never would, but he stayed prepared, and when his opportunity came, he seized it. Most people had written him off, but he had the utmost faith in himself and his abilities, staying true to his practice and talent.

Jeremy's success came with a lot of pressure, but he always handled it with grace and humility, never letting the stardom get to him and still showing up for his team.

Jeremy's story may not have had a storybook ending, but it definitely had its shiny moments, which will definitely follow Jeremy.

There are many lessons we can learn from this story. Jeremy always had it challenging. There was no paved road for him to walk through, and he had to work twice as hard to get what others were getting. This applies to the world we live in today. It is sometimes unfair, but that doesn't mean that we should give up. Our opportunity will surely come, and what a shame it will be if we aren't prepared when it arrives.

The pain of hard work is easier to swallow than the pain of regret. Whatever it is, school, work, relationships, or careers, we must persevere in the face of hardship because success is always just around the corner.

Another thing to remember is that change is the only constant thing in life. Whether we like it or not, seasons change, moments change, life changes. For Jeremy, he had a meteoric rise in fame for a few months, and then injuries hit him. We always have to remain grounded in the midst of this because we can be very quickly swept away. Surround yourself with people who support you, see and understand your vision, and will continue to root for you even when your seasons change, good or bad.

Even when your expectations are cut short, remain steadfast in your efforts, believing your time will come. The stories of people who persevered and achieved breakthroughs are endless. Believe in yourself.

During those years, Jeremy Lin spent time on the sidelines, overlooked and ignored, hated and stereotyped, and mistaken as a team trainer. When he had to sleep on his friend's couch because he couldn't afford his own apartment while being overlooked over and over again, he never would've imagined how Linsanity would reshape the world and change his life, but he also never doubted himself. Continue to believe in yourself, even when no one else does.

ACTIVITY

Take some time to answer these questions, and invite an adult to help you.

- Have you ever had an unexpected opportunity come your way? How did you respond, and what was the outcome?
- Think about something you love to do. Do you have people with similar backgrounds to look up to? Jeremy has become this for Asian basketball players.
- Reflect on a recent challenge or setback. Write down how you can turn it into an opportunity for growth inspired by Jeremy Lin's perseverance.

CHAPTER ELEVEN
TIM DUNCAN: THE BIG FUNDAMENTAL

"Good, better, best. Never let it rest. Until your good is better and your better is best."

—TIM DUNCAN

When you think of the most popular superstars that come to mind, the name Tim Duncan might not be at the top of your head. That's fair because Tim is known as a very quiet and humble player who never asks for the spotlight. However, he is one of the greatest forwards ever and was the primary force behind one of the most famous dynasties in the NBA, and he did it all without any flashy moves. His story is unique, and his love for sports did not start on the court; it actually began in the water.

Timothy Theodore Duncan was born in Saint Croix, US Virgin Islands, on April 25, 1976. Tim's parents were William and Ione Duncan. William worked as a mason, and Ione was a midwife. Tim has two older sisters and an older brother. His sisters, Cheryl and Tricia, were both great swimmers. Cheryl was a champion swimmer, and Tricia swam for the US Virgin Islands at the 1988

Summer Olympics held in Seoul. Tim's brother, Scott, is a film director and cinematographer. He's worked on numerous projects, including projects for ESPN, Fox Sports, NBC Sports, and Nickelodeon, to name a few.

As a child, Tim wanted to be like his sisters, so he learned to swim and became very good at it. As a teenager, he was so good that he became a standout swimmer in high school and dreamed of swimming in the 1992 Olympics. However, a hurricane destroyed the Olympic-sized pool in the US Virgin Islands, where Tim regularly trained. To keep training, he tried swimming in the ocean but quickly gave up because he was afraid of sharks. This led him to give up his dream of swimming in the Olympics.

After giving up on swimming, he turned his attention to another sport, basketball. Unfortunately, his mother passed away from breast cancer while he was only fourteen years old, but before her death, he promised her he would go to college and graduate. He fell into depression after she died, and his brother-in-law introduced him to basketball to break him out of his depressive state.

Tim had little natural talent. He was awkward on the court and wasn't very good at first. However, he kept playing and eventually got better and better. He got good enough to play for St. Dunstan's Episcopal High School, which was where his skills as a basketball player were first noticed. As a high school senior, he scored an average of twenty-five points per game, which helped him get noticed by a few colleges.

In 1992, Chris King and a group of NBA players traveled to the US Virgin Islands for a charity event. Among those players was Alonzo Mourning, a star center in the NBA at the time. Mourning was matched up against sixteen-year-old Tim Duncan in a scrimmage. Tim dominated Mourning on the court with his simple but consistent bank shot, impressing everyone around him.

When Chris returned home to Wake Forest, he told his coach about a tall, skinny, sixteen-year-old kid with great hands who dominated an NBA player on the court. Tim was offered a full scholarship to play college basketball for Wake Forest.

His exceptional skills and poise gained him national attention. His all-around play made him a standout prospect, and after his junior year, he was predicted to be the first draft pick of the NBA. However, he chose to stay in school for one more year to complete his degree in psychology, fulfilling his mother's dream for him to graduate from college. He won several awards playing college basketball and was now ready for the NBA draft.

The San Antonio Spurs held the first pick in the 1997 NBA Draft thanks to an injury-riddled 1996–97 season. They chose Tim Duncan with their pick, and the rest is history. Tim averaged 21.1 points per game as a rookie and was just behind the team's star center, David Robinson's 21.6 points per game. He also led the Spurs in rebounds per game with 11.9. In the 1997–98 season, Tim was named Rookie of the Year.

Tim and David Robinson formed an unbeatable duo known as the Twin Towers. Together, they dominated both ends of the court, creating a formidable frontcourt presence. Nobody could stop them from scoring in the paint, and nobody could score against them in the paint. In only his second year in the league, the Spurs would be led by Tim to the NBA Finals, where they would defeat the New York Knicks and secure the team's first-ever championship. Tim averaged twenty-four points and seventeen rebounds in his first of many NBA Finals. His remarkable performance earned him the Finals Most Valuable Player (FMVP). His contributions to his team went beyond his incredible playing skills. His leadership, consistency, and unselfishness were a massive part of the Spurs' successes over the years.

Tim was famous for his fundamental playing style and consistency in his performance. He was a reliable player every game and every season. His scoring, rebounding, and defensive contributions never changed, earning him the respect of fans, teammates, and even his opponents.

His game was built on the fundamentals of basketball, which include dribbling, rebounding, passing, shooting, and footwork. He was a master of the basics, including footwork, timing, and positioning. He rarely made flashy plays but was always in the right spot, used simple moves that always worked, and got the job done. In addition to this, he led by example. Some of his teammates said he was not a super-vocal or demonstrative leader. Still, his work ethic, commitment, and selflessness caused his teammates to look up to him. These attributes, paired with his calm demeanor, led Shaquille O'Neal to give him the nickname "The Big Fundamental" for his dull, simple, yet incredibly effective style.

With his fundamental playing style and selfless leadership, the Spurs became an elite team for his entire career, showcasing high levels of teamwork and efficiency. By the time he retired, he had won five NBA Championships, was an NBA MVP twice, a Finals MVP three times, and played in fifteen All-Star games. He was never one to seek out the spotlight, interviews, or commercial endorsements. Yet, he is still widely known in the basketball community as one of the greatest to ever play.

LESSONS FROM TIM DUNCAN

One important lesson you should learn from Tim Duncan's career is the importance of mastering the basics and the fundamentals. This may not necessarily be the fundamentals of basketball but the fundamental skills of whatever path you choose for yourself.

Tim prioritized his team's success over himself. He prioritized scoring over flashy moves and focused on perfecting the basics. Even though he did not originally want to be a basketball player and was initially awkward on the court, his focus on the fundamental principles of the game catapulted him to dizzying heights.

What do you want to do? Do you want to be an artist, an athlete, a chef, or a scientist? Then, you must first understand and master the fundamental principles of that field.

Think of it like laying the foundation of a building. If the foundation is well laid, it is likely that the building will stay stable. The foundation of a one-story house is different from the foundation of a skyscraper. They are both buildings, but their foundations can carry different weights and handle different amounts of pressure. To become great at something, you must lay a rock-solid foundation of the basics and fundamentals. You don't need to be flashy like other players; Tim shows you that you can succeed with just the basics.

Despite being one of the greatest basketball players of his time, it is also important to note that Tim was humble and selfless. It is so important to be humble when you succeed. Many great and successful people lost everything they had in the blink of an eye due to pride. Pride makes you take unnecessary risks and prevents a person from seeing clearly. Pride results in people believing they can't make mistakes, which causes them to do just that.

Some athletes injured themselves while making unnecessary flashy plays that ended their careers or injured them. It is more important to play a game and survive to play another than to make a flashy play and never make another play again. Tim understood this, which was why he only sustained one major injury during his entire career.

This humility extended to his life outside of basketball. He was a major contributor to several cancer movements in honor of his mother and an amazing father and husband. This humility is what made Tim so respected among his peers. He never hesitated to help others get better and never tried to lift himself above them. Reading the accounts of his teammates will help you realize exactly how loved and respected he was for this.

One benefit of emulating Tim is his consistency. His ability to bring his best to every game at every season, regardless of what else was going on in his life at the time, is something that you should strive to copy. In all your pursuits, always bring your A game. Never do anything halfway, whether it's in sports, academics, or even your hobbies.

Whatever you want to do, ensure you master the basics first. It is like a math problem. You need to know basic addition before you can learn multiplication. Starting from the basics will ensure that complex techniques will be a piece of cake.

Mastering the basics will turn you into a superstar in whatever activity you choose. Focus on the fundamentals and spend time mastering them. Remember the ten thousand-hour rule; applying it while mastering the fundamentals will elevate your skill to the next level and keep you above your peers.

Do not only celebrate yourself but also celebrate anyone who helped you achieve those goals. This could be your parents, guardians, or teachers. Continue to learn and grow. Just because you have achieved your goal does not mean that it is the end of your journey. Set new goals for yourself and constantly improve your life.

Remember, you don't have to make flashy plays to succeed. Success is about talent, effort, attitude, and character. Tim Duncan might not be the most fancy player, but he is one of the most respected.

ACTIVITY

Take some time to answer these questions, and invite an adult to help you.

- Can you think of a time when you tried to be too fancy or flashy at something, and it worked against you?
- Choose a skill you want to develop. Create a plan to work on the basic elements of this skill, following Tim Duncan's example of dedication to fundamentals.

CHAPTER TWELVE

KLAY THOMPSON: OVERCOMING DEVASTATING INJURIES

"It's not the end of the road for me. I still know I have greatness ahead of me. This was the first full season in three years I've had to make it through start to finish healthy, so that's a positive, and I know I'm gonna come back even better next year."

—KLAY THOMPSON

K lay Thompson is a professional basketball player who plays for the Golden State Warriors in the NBA and is famous for "catching fire" in games and making three-point shots nonstop like there's no tomorrow. Despite his success, he has also suffered several horrible injuries, including a torn ACL (Anterior Cruciate Ligament) and torn Achilles tendon, which caused him to miss out on valuable time in his career. In this chapter, we will discuss how he overcame these challenges to make a comeback and how you can too.

Klay Alexander Thompson was born in Los Angeles, California, on February 8, 1990. His dad, Mychal Thompson, was the first draft pick of the NBA in 1978. His mother played volleyball for the

University of Portland and the University of San Francisco, so Klay was fortunate to grow up with athletic parents. Klay would eventually become known for his pure shooting form, which, surprisingly, he did not get from his dad, who played center in the NBA. Klay credits his former coach, Dr. Kaempf, for teaching him the fundamentals of shooting the basketball.

When Klay was fourteen, his family moved to Ladera Ranch, California, where he graduated from Santa Margarita Catholic High School. In his junior season, he was named to the All-Area second team and the Orange County third team. This means he was one of the best players in his local area. As a senior, he scored an average of twenty-one points per game and led his team to a Division 3 State Championship appearance. During the State Championship, Klay set a finals record of seven three-pointers in a game, which was only a preview of much more to come. Given his high school success, he would play basketball for Washington State University.

As a freshman at Washington State University, he started all thirty-three games that season. He scored the most three-pointers and free throws in the team, scoring an average of 12.5 points per game. He was named to the Pac-10 All-Freshman team. As a sophomore, Klay had an amazing sophomore year season. He broke the great Alaska shootout record, reaching 1000 points. This earned him all Pac-10 First-Team honors and Player of the Week. Making it to the first team means the player is the best of the best. As a junior, Thompson was the top scorer in the Pac-10. He won more first-team and player-of-the-week awards and set several Washington State University records for most points in a game, most points in a season, and most points in a career. His jersey was retired by Washington State University in 2020, which means that no other player will ever wear that jersey number again. He was the seventh athlete in all sports to receive this honor.

After graduating from college, he was drafted by the Warriors as the eleventh overall pick in the 2011 NBA draft. Klay quickly established himself as a very productive shooter and a major part of the Warrior's core team, along with Stephen Curry and Draymond Green. He and Curry formed the "Splash Brothers" duo, setting several records for combined three-pointers in a season. During the first several years of his career, he did some unthinkable things. Klay once scored thirty-seven points in a single quarter without missing a single shot. He has scored sixty points in a game while only taking eleven dribbles. He holds the record for most three-pointers in a game (fourteen) and most three-pointers in a playoff game (eleven).

He is known for having great performances in games that matter most, especially in game 6 situations. Game 6 is the part of a playoff series where one team is at risk of being eliminated; it can be one of the most intense games of the series. In 2016, the Warriors were in a game 6 and at risk of being eliminated by the Oklahoma City Thunder, and this is where Thompson scored forty-one points and made eleven three-pointers to beat the record.

After an amazing run and multiple championships, disaster would come to Klay. During the 2019 NBA Finals series between the Raptors and the Warriors, there was another game 6 where Klay was beginning to take over. Unfortunately, Klay tore his ACL during the game and would have to leave. With an injury like this, a player must take at least one year to recover and return to the game. Klay had never been troubled by an injury like this before.

A year later, in late 2020, Klay was almost ready to return to the court when another disaster struck. During practice, he tore his Achilles tendon, which also takes a year or more to recover from.

Imagine spending a whole year recovering and being so close to returning, only to start over again.

2020 and 2021 should have been some of the most important years of Klay's career as a basketball player. Still, due to his injuries, he could not even walk, let alone play competitive basketball. He had to endure months of painful rehabilitation. However, instead of being sad and blaming his circumstances, Klay said that smooth waters do not make a great sailor. This was a way of saying that hardships and adversity make someone better. He focused on getting better in rehab and eventually returned to the court.

Several of his close friends described the period as "dark days." They said that Klay battled severe trauma from those injuries and experienced periods of depression. It's tough not being able to do something you love and have it taken away due to a physical disability. Think of the last time you were sick and could not go outside to play with your friends. How did you feel watching them play without you? That feeling was the same thing Klay felt for almost a year while recovering from his injuries.

His dark days would end, and in early 2022, Klay Thompson would return to the court again and rejoin his teammates on the Golden State Warriors. Not only that, but he would help them win the 2022 NBA Championship only months after returning. He continues to have great performances and show off his amazing shooting ability. Although it was not an easy road, and it's still difficult to always play how he used to, he never lets that stop him from doing what he loves.

LESSONS FROM KLAY THOMPSON

Klay climbed to the mountaintop of success and quickly had it collapse. A torn Achilles tendon is a career-ruining injury for an athlete. Because the Achilles tendon is one of the most important muscles in running, walking, and jumping, tearing means the person may be unable to walk. Klay did not let this dissuade him; instead, he focused on learning to walk, run, and jump again. He had to go back to the beginning and relearn how to be a great basketball player. He described it as the worst moment of his life.

He had to reinvent himself to build himself up again from scratch. To express his competitive spirit, he learned how to swim and drive a boat. After about two and a half long years away from the court, Klay was finally able to return.

This was only possible because of his resilience. Remember how we said resilience is the ability to get back up when you fall? Klay was able to do that. He sustained two devastating injuries that would have ended the careers of other athletes. Still, he was able to pick himself up and keep going. He was determined to get back on the court and took steps to go to rehab to make it happen.

Getting back up from trouble is a process that takes time. The process of recovery for Klay took two and a half years. That is a really long time, especially when you aren't able to do what you love. He was forced to exercise patience and perseverance. When he had surgery on his leg, his parents took him to their house to take care of him. His friends were all around him to support and cheer him up. He surrounded himself with people who would keep him happy and cheerful and encourage him. Perseverance is the ability to continue even when all hope seems lost. That was what Klay did. Several doctors told him he wouldn't be able to play basketball again, and some even told him he wouldn't run again.

But he kept at it until he walked until he ran, and until he jumped again.

In life, there will be times when you experience challenges. They may be physical or emotional, but always keep your head up. Don't be afraid of challenges; instead, face them head-on. Look in the mirror and tell yourself I am stronger than this; I will beat this and win. Then, make a plan. What can you do to resolve your issue? Once you make your plan, follow it, stick to it, and you will overcome it.

Stay positive. No matter what. Always remind yourself of things you should be thankful for. Wake up in the morning and be grateful to be awake. Be grateful for your fingers and your toes. Gracefulness helps you recognize what you have, and knowing that you have something makes you happy. When Klay got hurt, it made him appreciate and cherish playing competitive basketball even more. Sometimes, you don't realize how amazing something is until it's gone. Even when everything seems tough, always look on the bright side. Tell yourself that no matter how dark it gets at night, the sun always comes out in the morning. And no matter how hard things get, you will make it through.

Always listen to your parents and teachers. They will always want the best for you and try to guide you down the right path. When you are not sure of what steps to take, go to them and ask them. They are wise and will definitely help you.

Never stay down. Even if you tumble and fall, always get back up. Be resilient, just like Klay.

ACTIVITY

Take some time to answer these questions, and invite an adult to help you.

- Have you ever gotten injured? If so, how difficult was the recovery for you?
- What is something you currently love doing? What can you do to appreciate and cherish it more, gaining inspiration from how Klay loves basketball even more since recovering from his injuries

CHAPTER THIRTEEN

WILT CHAMBERLAIN: A RECORD THAT HAS STOOD THE TEST OF TIME

"Everybody pulls for David, nobody roots for Goliath."

—WILT CHAMBERLAIN

In the history of basketball, many players were overlooked for most of their lives. There were also many players who people thought had great potential. Wilt Chamberlain wasn't just looked at as having great potential; everybody knew he would dominate basketball. At just ten years old, he already stood six feet tall. He often referred to himself as Goliath on the court. Although it's helpful to be tall in basketball, you still need to do the right things to become great. Wilt did that and went on to hold the greatest record ever.

Wilt Chamberlain was born on August 21, 1936, in Philadelphia, Pennsylvania, as one of his parent's nine children. That's right, he had eight brothers and sisters. Somewhat surprisingly, Wilt was not the biggest fan of basketball, saying it was a "game for sissies." But he was from Philly, a state where basketball was super popular and an integral part of the culture and society. Thanks to this, he found his way to the court, and thus, his love for the game began.

In 1953, he started attending the Shoemaker Junior High School and joined the basketball team. Wilt's skills quickly became apparent, gaining momentum and recognition, which grew as he went to Overbrook High School. During his time on the Overbrook Hilltoppers basketball team, his height gave him an edge and a natural advantage over the other players, setting him apart. He was already well over six feet, a towering Goliath on the court! Not long after, he became well-known for his scoring talent, physical strength, and shot-blocking abilities.

In 1955, Wilt's skills brought him under the radar of college scouts, and he received a scholarship to Kansas University to play for the Kansas Jayhawks, a team he particularly loved and held dear to his heart. During his time at Kansas, Wilt matched and shattered numerous records and earned accolades, including being named the NCAA Final Four Most Outstanding Player in 1957. His dominance on the court was matched only by his larger-than-life personality. Wilt was well-known as a team player and quickly became a favorite wherever he went.

Unfortunately, in his sophomore year, his team lost the National Championship game to the North Carolina Tar Heels in triple overtime. Wilt expressed many times over the years that he felt personally responsible for this loss and made it his mission to become not just better but the best. He used his loss as fuel for his goals and began to work hard. Remember other players who did this?

Before he began his career in the NBA, Wilt became one of the first players to play for the Harlem Globetrotters, a team outside of the NBA that mainly combined entertainment, comedy, theater, and basketball. They're a popular team now, but Wilt pioneered that.

Wilt would then start playing for the NBA in 1959, where he played for the Philadelphia / San Francisco Warriors, Philadelphia 76ers, and Los Angeles Lakers. There was no doubt that Wilt Chamberlain was a star player. During his career, he averaged a crazy thirty points and twenty-two rebounds per game. However, the one thing that would cement Wilt as one of the greatest in history was when he set a record for most points in a single game. Against the New York Knicks in 1962, Wilt scored 100 points. This feat was, at the time, one of a kind; Wilt had shattered the world record, placing him among the top five players in the world. This remarkable feat, which stands as the NBA record for most points scored in a game even to this day, cemented Wilt's legacy as one of the greatest scorers in basketball history. Beyond the sheer numbers, this accomplishment symbolized Wilt's unparalleled determination and ability to rise to the occasion when the odds seemed insurmountable.

His personal brilliance notwithstanding, Wilt was always on the hunt for team success. He wanted his team on the map, and he was not afraid to go up against other giants of the game to make it happen. Throughout his career, he played against formidable opponents, including the legendary Bill Russell with his Boston Celtics dynasty. They would have many legendary battles, but despite Wilt's best efforts, he often found himself on the losing end of them, with Russell's Celtics emerging victorious repeatedly in the NBA Finals. After all, Bill Russell won thirteen NBA Championships. These defeats were painful reminders of the harsh realities of competition and the importance of resilience in adversity. You can't always win; sometimes, you will lose more than you win. Although the defeats were painful, Wilt did not give up.

Apart from being an exceptional player, Wilt was also a remarkable human being, as expressed by many of his peers and mentors. He was driven, focused, and always on the move to be better. Wilt, however skilled he was, wasn't perfect; he had a tough time making free throws, but this did not discourage him as a player. Rather than accept it as a weakness, he decided to try shooting free throws underhanded rather than overhand like everyone else. It actually worked and made Wilt's free-throw percentage a bit better. Sometimes, you must try something different that might work for you.

By the time Wilt retired in 1973, he had two NBA Championships, four MVP awards, a Finals MVP, and several other awards, including All-Star appearances. After all these years, he still holds the record for the most rebounds in a career at 23,924. The only person to beat his career points per game is Michael Jordan. His 100-point record has yet to be broken, with the closest person being Kobe Bryant at eighty-one. Wilt played in the earliest era of the NBA compared to the rest of the players we've discussed, and he represents such a foundational and historical piece to how the NBA was played back in those years. He was a pioneer and trailblazer who still holds many records decades later.

LESSONS FROM WILT CHAMBERLAIN

It is clear from this story that Wilt Chamberlain never settled for mediocrity, which means he did not want to be just average or decent. He had great ambition and work ethic. The player continued to train and improve himself constantly, never feeling too proud to ask for help when needed. It is worth copying in your own life. Never settle for average when you have what it takes to be the best. Even if you are naturally gifted in a field, that doesn't rule out the place of training and hard work because a seed that is not well watered and nurtured will die.

On the other hand, Wilt was fortunate to find something he was naturally gifted at and built to do. For him, that was basketball, so he combined natural gifts with hard work. After all, he was six feet tall at a young age. This is something we can do, too. Everyone has their natural gifts; we can find our gifts and see if we can become great at them as Wilt did.

We can also see that Wilt was not content with being just a shot blocker or a scoring talent; he wanted to be an all-around player and worked hard to achieve that. His coach, Dolph Schayes, said, "Wilt wanted to be the best at everything." Schayes added, "If you talked bowling with Wilt, he'd say, 'I'm the best bowler you've ever seen. If I was to box (Muhammad) Ali, I'd beat the heck out of him. If I was on track, I'd be the fastest guy.'" He was never satisfied with being in his comfort zone; instead, he constantly pushed himself to become something better. This is usually an uncomfortable process.

Wilt was a beacon of hope, not just to other players but to the young boys on the courts of Philadelphia, who didn't get the same opportunities as him. Posters of him hung on bedroom walls. Many admired his resilience on and off the court, and he became a role model for many. He wasn't the Goliath out to destroy David and the Israelites; he was the Goliath who led the way with his strength. He was the Goliath who pioneered a new professional league of basketball stars, all because he followed his talents and dreams.

Chamberlain lived a purposeful life, setting goals for himself and working hard to achieve them. This still applies today: Find your vision, write it down, and set smaller goals to help achieve the bigger one. It is also important to have personal boundaries, lines you will not cross, and rules you will live by. All of this helped Chamberlain become who he was, and they will continue to be relevant tools in achieving any goal.

It's easy to set goals that apply to your vision. Here's an example:

As a student, if you want to get all A's, that's a vision, right? Start by setting smaller goals like these;

- Study for at least five hours a day.
- Make sure to attend all classes.
- Get a tutor, someone better than you, and learn from that person.
- Prepare adequately for tests and assignments.
- Pass the exams.

These might seem like little things, but when done properly, they will help you achieve the overall goal of making all A's.

If you encounter limitations or situations you feel are bigger than your abilities, seek help. If Wilt Chamberlain was able to do it, you can too. Maybe you don't have the same gift of height that he had, but you have some gift within you. Find that gift and cherish it. Talk to people who have done what you are trying to do, study them, and invest time in reading, learning, and growing stronger.

Everything is only possible once someone does it. Don't be afraid to try something new, don't be afraid to reach high and dream big, but, more importantly, be willing to do the work it takes to make those dreams come true.

ACTIVITY

Take some time to answer these questions, and invite an adult to help you.

- What are some natural gifts or interests you have? Like Wilt's height and basketball gifts, you, too, have your own gifts.
- Think of a goal you believe is challenging to achieve. What steps can you take to work toward it, inspired by Chamberlain's pursuit of excellence?
- Identify a personal record you would like to set or break. Plan out how you will work toward this goal. Just like how Wilt always beat his scoring records

CHAPTER FOURTEEN

THE 2004 DETROIT PISTONS: THE UNDERDOGS TRIUMPH

"All the successful teams I've ever seen have three characteristics: They play unselfishly, they play together, and they play hard."

—LARRY BROWN

Just like we can find lessons and inspirations in the stories of players, we also find them in the stories of entire teams and what they could do. After all, basketball is a team sport. There are not many stories of victory in basketball history that are as unexpected and surprising as the story of the 2004 Detroit Pistons. This team defied all odds, overcoming challenges and doubts to achieve the ultimate victory: winning the NBA Championship against a scary and mighty opponent, the Los Angeles Lakers.

The 2004 NBA Finals was a stage set for an epic showdown between two very different teams. On one side stood the star-studded Lakers, led by future Hall of Famer Kobe Bryant and his fellow superstar, Shaquille O'Neal. With their player roster boasting some of the most famous names in the sport, the Lakers were widely considered the favorites to win the championship, and it was a no-brainer that they would once again win it all.

On the other side stood the Detroit Pistons, a team known more for their tough defense and team-oriented style of play rather than individual superstars. This team was a typical example of strength in numbers. The team was led by head coach Larry Brown and anchored by players like Chauncey Billups, Ben Wallace, Rip Hamilton, Rasheed Wallace, and Tayshaun Prince. They were great players but less famous than the other team's superstar names. The Pistons were the symbol of an underdog team. An underdog team is a team that is not expected to win or has a lower chance of winning. As a team, they had become used to the doubts and being ranked as unlikely to win. Still, just as in our favorite movies where the underdogs come out on top in the end, this team of underdogs was determined to flip to the next chapter.

The Pistons' road to the championship began long before the 2004 season. After years of unimpressive performances in the NBA, the team went through a significant transformation in the early 2000s. In 2000, the Pistons hired legendary coach Larry Brown, a tenacious man known for his ability to instill discipline and defensive prowess in his teams. Under Brown's leadership, the Pistons began to adopt a team-oriented style of play that prioritized defense and selflessness over individual glory.

Coach Larry was able to identify each player's strengths and implement them in the general strategy of play. Still, despite their talent and chemistry, the Pistons were not considered serious contenders for the NBA Championship at the start of the 2003–2004 season.

The Pistons proved everyone wrong by having a stellar regular season. Their team-oriented style of play, which was previously overlooked, earned them a 54–28 record and a place as the third seed in the East for the NBA playoffs. The moment of truth for the Pistons' playoff run came in the Eastern Conference Finals against the Indiana Pacers, the number one seed. In a grueling seven-game series, the Pistons were pitted against a Pacers team led by All-Star forward Jermaine O'Neal and defensive menace Ron Artest. The series was marked by intense physicality and defensive battles, with neither team willing to give an inch. Ultimately, the Pistons' resilience and determination carried them to victory, as they emerged victorious in the final game 7 to advance to the NBA Finals for the first time since 1990.

The war did not end there for them, as they were prepared to face off against the star-studded Los Angeles Lakers in the NBA Finals. The Pistons entered the series as heavy underdogs, while the Lakers had already made a name for themselves with their remarkable talents.

However, these inspiring underdogs would not go down without a fight. With their trademark defensive system, which left little room for the one-two punch of Kobe and Shaq from the Lakers, and their selfless offense, the Pistons stunned the basketball world by defeating the Lakers in game one. The victory was a testament to the Pistons' collective will and determination, proving team-work and selflessness could overcome individual talent and star power.

As the series progressed, it became increasingly clear that the Pistons were not just competing with the Lakers—they were out playing them. With each victory, their confidence grew, while doubts began to creep into the minds of the Lakers' players and fans alike. In a stunning turn of events, the Pistons clinched the NBA Championship in five games, defeating the Lakers in a decisive game 5 to capture their first title since 1990. The victory was a testament to the Pistons' resilience, determination, and unwavering belief in themselves.

But it wasn't just their defense that propelled the Pistons to victory; their unselfishness and teamwork set them apart. Unlike the Lakers, whose offense was primarily driven around Kobe Bryant and Shaquille O'Neal, the Pistons relied on contributions from every player on the roster. Chauncey Billups emerged as the team's leader, earning the NBA Finals MVP award for his clutch performances and unwavering leadership.

It was the underdog story of the decade. Not many teams in NBA history can defy expectations and overcome elite teams. The Los Angeles Lakers had already won three championships in a row in recent years. They were a dynasty, and it would have been silly for anybody to bet against them. However, the Detroit Pistons had faith in themselves and made the seemingly impossible happen.

LESSONS FROM THE 2004 DETROIT PISTONS

From this story, we can gather that the players of the Detroit Pistons were not selfish; they lived by the phrase "teamwork makes the dream work." While seemingly unimpressive as individual players, their combined strengths made them a dominant force in the NBA. All of the experts in the NBA had already decided that they were not a team that would challenge for the NBA Championship.

The team may not have had superstars like Kobe or Shaq, but it had team players—players who were ready and willing to take one for the team. Together, they found a way to harness their individual talents into something greater. These players weren't selfishly trying to bring glory for themselves; they weren't trying to prove to anyone that the NBA had made a mistake by not believing in them; they simply wanted to show up for each other, and in doing that, they showed the world.

Sometimes, you might be tempted to leave the team behind and pursue self-glory. Still, we must remember that whatever you think you can achieve alone, you can achieve much more with the help of a team working alongside you. There's no success or stardom in one person succeeding while the rest of the team fails; that counteracts the point of being in a team. Teammates show up and show out for each other, regardless of personal goals or desires. It is selflessly putting the good of the team first.

It doesn't matter what capacity you find yourself in; when you are on a team, be a team player. It could be a sports team, a family game night, or a school project. Whatever it may be, remember that there's no "I" in the team. Be willing to help even the weaker ones or ask for help if needed because everyone will be judged by the team's collective strength, not by their personal achievements.

Working in teams has a lot to do with communication, respect, and the willingness to learn and grow together. It is not always the easiest to work with different people. Still, you must understand that each person, even as unlikely as it may seem, has something to offer for the general good of the team. Be patient enough to find out what. And if you ever find yourself on an underdog team, remember the movies where the weakest teams came out on top. Keep going, and be willing to work hard to prove the doubters wrong.

Another key part of the 2004 Detroit Pistons was how they were doubted and overlooked. Sometimes in life, you or your team might be doubted and ignored in the same way. Some people may think you won't win that sports game or won't do the best in your class on a school project. Don't buy into those negative comments. Believe in yourself and your team that you can get the job done and win any competition. The first step to making something happen is believing you can do it. It might not be easy, and it might require hard work but don't believe anyone who tells you it's impossible.

You can imagine you have a piece of paper. It's easy to tear that piece of paper since it's thin and not strong on its own. However, when you get ten or twenty pieces of paper stacked together like a team, it is much harder to tear all the paper. You probably won't be able to do it. This happens when you become part of a team that works together. Life and difficulties will come and try to tear you, but if you stay united with your team, family, and community, you can't be torn. So, choose to be selfless and support the team before your own personal glory.

ACTIVITY

Take some time to answer these questions, and invite an adult to help you.

- Have you been part of a team where you accomplished something when some people thought you couldn't, just like the Detroit Pistons?
- Does your confidence stay strong even when many people begin to doubt you?
- Discuss a time when you were part of a team that helped you achieve more than you could alone.

CHAPTER FIFTEEN
THE REDEEM TEAM: A 2008 OLYMPICS REDEMPTION STORY

"(Beijing) 2008 was about reclaiming what we started. We couldn't wait to get after it and challenge for that gold medal... for us it was a shot at redemption."

—KOBE BRYANT

There may be stories of players and teams who overcome the odds to achieve great things, but there are also stories of players and teams who fall short and experience big disappointments. This will happen to almost everybody. The key is what you do next. In this chapter, we'll learn about a great story of redemption and making up for past failures.

While the 2004 championships were a source of celebration for the Detroit Pistons, it was a tough time for the United States Men's Olympic basketball team, a wake-up call they did not know they needed. During every Olympics, the best and brightest stars in the NBA come together to play for the United States Olympic team and try to bring home the gold medal for the country. The NBA is home to the greatest players in the world, so the gold medal was expected.

Despite being favorites to win gold in 2004, as usual, they had to settle for not even silver but bronze, which left the entire country in shock and surprise. It was a stark reminder that individual talent alone was not enough to guarantee success at the highest level of competition and that something needed to change.

After the team's disappointing performance in the 2004 Olympics, the team decided it was time to change tactics. Taking a page from our favorite underdogs, they embarked on a journey of renewed focus on teamwork, striving for dedication, and the renewal of their national pride. They decided that a big mindset and culture change was in order. The Olympics was not just a casual tournament; it was a privilege to play for your country. Mike Krzyzewski, the new head coach, made it a point of emphasis to teach the players about what it means to play as an American. He would show them images and videos to teach them about the country's history.

This formation of the revised 2008 team marked a significant shift in mindset, with players prioritizing the collective goal of representing their country with distinction rather than putting the focus on personal glory. The NBA's greatest stars would prioritize being part of this effort. This new team was led by all-stars and seasoned veterans of the sport, with Kobe Bryant being the team's captain. Kobe did not play in the 2004 Olympics, so he was determined to make up for it. Kobe was paired alongside stars like LeBron James, Dwyane Wade, Chris Paul, and many others. Kobe brought a sense of leadership and desire to his teammates, reportedly saying, "I'm tired of watching y'all lose."

This new and improved 2008 team embraced a culture of friendship and teamwork from the beginning. They took their previous defeat as a learning session, a spotlight on all the areas they needed to work on. A distinctive characteristic of this team was their willingness to work on their perceived weaknesses and make the changes necessary to get the results they wanted. These players understood that their individual greatness would only truly shine when harnessed within the framework of a cohesive team.

The process of forming the 2008 team was meticulous and deliberate. Each player was expected to possess defining characteristics; it wouldn't be business as usual. Players were selected for their skill, athleticism, and willingness to buy into the team-first ethos that coach Mike Krzyzewski sought to instill; with each player committing to putting the team's success above their personal search for glory, a formidable roster emerged, ready to redeem themselves and take on the world. After all, this team would bring glory back to US basketball after the crushing 2004 defeat. This gave the team the nickname "The Redeem Team."

The 2008 Beijing Olympics set the stage for the Redeem Team to showcase their renewed focus and accomplish their goal. From the opening tip-off of the first group stage games, it was clear that this was a team on a mission; the players knew they had been robbed of their rightful place at the top of the basketball pyramid. They were more than determined to earn their spot back. They defeated opponents in the group stages by twenty, thirty, and even fifty points. They played with a sense of purpose and intensity, driven by the desire to reclaim their rightful place atop the basketball world.

Throughout the tournament, the US team faced formidable opponents; they weren't the only ones to up their game in the last four years. Each of the teams they faced presented its own unique challenges. But the US team, armed with its new code of ethics, newfound team spirit, and goal to redeem itself, pushed through each phase of the competition, slowly but steadily defeating its opponents, displaying a level of dominance that matched the glory days of US basketball.

Key players like Kobe and LeBron rose to the occasion time and again, delivering clutch performances when it mattered most. As team leaders, they motivated the players to push themselves to heights never seen before. Their leadership, both on and off the court, served as a guiding light, inspiring their teammates to do their best for the good of the entire team.

The gold medal grew closer with each game the US team played and won, but the competition also leveled up. It eventually reached its peak in the final match. The US team faced off against Spain in the gold medal game. Spain would prove to be a formidable opponent, and the game had viewers worldwide on the edge of their seats and crossing their fingers. It was a fitting finale to an incredible journey, with two basketball powerhouses battling it out for Olympic supremacy. But on this day, the US team emerged victorious by defeating Spain 118–107. Their commitment to teamwork and dedication to the country shined through as they claimed the gold medal with a resounding victory.

It was a glorious day, not just for the players but for the country as a whole. The country had put their faith in the team and were rewarded. The 2008 Beijing Olympics marked a turning point for the US men's basketball team, signaling a return to dominance on the international stage. Through their commitment to teamwork and national pride, they overcame adversity and reclaimed their rightful place with the gold medal. It was a moment of redemption, not just for the players but for basketball fans across the country who had stood by their team through triumph and tribulation.

LESSONS FROM THE 2008 REDEEM TEAM

The 2008 Redeem Team set a new bar for years to come. The gold medal is the expectation of every Olympic team from here on out. Of course, their previous loss must've stung; it would have hurt their pride to lose to another country that shouldn't have beaten them, the so-called underdogs. Imagine being the best at something where everyone knows you are an undefeated champion in this particular thing, but then, out of nowhere, some unknown person with no championships comes in and defeats you. It sends a shockwave through your body; it can make you question your abilities, make you doubt yourself, and wonder if you are as good as you thought or even good enough.

These players faced this in the 2004 Olympics; they didn't just disappoint the country; they disappointed themselves. But that did not keep them down. Was it disappointing? Yes. Was it demoralizing? Probably. But that did not mean they locked themselves in the bedroom to feel sorry for themselves. While it is important to take the time to mourn a loss, it is even more vital to know when to get up, dust yourself up, and get moving.

There's a saying, "Success has many friends, but failure is an orphan." Nobody wants to be around failure, but it is a part of life. You try, and you fail. Then you try again, and maybe you fail again. It might take you several attempts to succeed. But there's always another chance for you to recover from your failure and go after success. The most important thing is that you get back up.

We explored in the previous chapter how important teamwork is; it truly cannot be overemphasized because, in the same way, these players would not have been able to emerge victorious had they tried to do it just trying to take control as individual stars. In the same way, we need the help of others if we are to achieve our goals because the truth is, there are some obstacles we cannot cross alone. Success is rarely achieved in isolation. By working together toward a common goal and leveraging each other's strengths, teams can achieve more than individual accomplishments.

Achieving excellence requires unwavering dedication and commitment to the task at hand. The members of the 2008 Redeem Team demonstrated their commitment to representing their country with distinction, putting in the hard work and sacrifice necessary to succeed, even if they had to put their egos to the side. Remember, these players were all the stars of their own NBA teams and the best players in the world. The fact that all of these players put their egos aside to work together as a team is a really big deal.

Another lesson from this story is that strong leadership is essential for guiding a team toward success. Players like Kobe Bryant, LeBron James, and Dwyane Wade provided leadership on and off the court, inspiring their teammates to elevate their game and embody the values of teamwork. Kobe especially brought an edge and influence to the team, which got them in the right mindset. Look for a mentor, someone you can look up to and respect, someone you can trust to always guide you in the right direction. Develop your leadership skills so that you can help your future teams.

Representing one's country on the international stage is a privilege and an honor. The players on the 2008 Redeem Team embraced this opportunity with pride, recognizing the significance of wearing their country's colors and competing for something greater than themselves. If you ever find yourself called on to represent your country, recognize that it is a privilege and treat it as such. Let your nation's pride come before your own, and in doing that, you ultimately bring pride to yourself.

ACTIVITY

Take some time to answer these questions, and invite an adult to help you.

- Share your own story of when you got a second chance. How did it impact you? What lesson did you learn?
- Learn about your country's history and why someone would be proud to represent their country in their career like NBA players do.
- Identify a past mistake or failure. Reflect on what you learned from it and how you can use that experience to improve in a current or future endeavor.

CONCLUSION

We've reached the end of this book! The final buzzer has sounded. This has been an incredible journey, and I hope some of these stories have resonated with you, showing that even the greatest players started out as kids like you, facing their own challenges and creating a path for themselves.

It might have looked like Kobe Bryant's Mamba Mentality, Tim Duncan's humble approach, or Lisa Leslie's pioneering attitude— but these players found their passion and left a mark in their unique ways. They always remembered that hard work was the key to true success, and so should you. Whatever you want to do, even if it's not basketball, remember that you have the potential for greatness if you practice the same work ethic.

Whether it was being doubted and overlooked like Stephen Curry, growing up with no money like LeBron James, or carrying the pressure of gold medal expectations like the Redeem Team—these players and teams experienced challenges they had to overcome. Challenges where they could have failed, and sometimes they did, but they never stopped trying and proving people wrong. Challenges will come, and life will be hard, but never give up.

Now, it's your turn to write your story. You are just at the beginning and have a world of possibilities in front of you. Take your time to find your passions and figure out what you can do to become more like these basketball legends. Take those extra hours to study to do better in school. Have the courage to start a new hobby even if you may not be good at first. Find who your supporters and mentors are and learn from them. Just get better every day and keep your head high even when things don't go your way. You've got this; I'm rooting for you!

You've dribbled through every page and scored knowledge on every chapter—now you're ready to pass the ball and help keep the game of basketball alive for others!

Having you and your parents leave an honest review of this book on Amazon is like making the assist that wins the game. It shows other young players where they can find the tips, stories, and inspiration they need to play their best game.

Basketball is more than just a game; it's a community of players, fans, and dreamers passing their passion and knowledge forward. By sharing your thoughts, you become a crucial part of this community.

Thank you for helping us keep the love for basketball thriving. Every review helps, and yours means the world to us.

Scan the QR code below to leave your review on Amazon.

Your support not only spreads the joy of basketball but also keeps the spirit of the game alive. You're not just a reader; you're a true game changer!

- From all of us who love the game

REFERENCES

National Geographic Kids. (n.d.). Bonkers about basketball! Retrieved from https://www.natgeokids.com/uk/kids-club/entertainment/general-entertainment/bonkers-about-basketball/

Growing Play. (2023, March 20). 20 fun basketball facts for kids. Retrieved from https://www.growingplay.com/2023/03/20-fun-basketball-facts-for-kids/

Red Bull. (n.d.). Basketball facts. Retrieved from https://www.redbull.com/us-en/basketball-facts

The Indian Express. (n.d.). 'I've failed over and over and over again in my life and that is why I succeed': Michael Jordan motivational video. Retrieved from https://indianexpress.com/article/lifestyle/life-positive/ive-failed-over-and-over-and-over-again-in-my-life-and-that-is-why-i-succeed-michael-jordan-motivational-video-7839233/

23Jordan.com. (n.d.). Bio. Retrieved from https://www.23jordan.com/bio

Biography.com. (n.d.). Michael Jordan: Life before NBA, early career. Retrieved from https://www.biography.com/athletes/michael-jordan-life-before-nba-early-career

Notable Biographies. (n.d.). Jordan, Michael. Retrieved from https://www.notablebiographies.com/Jo-Ki/Jordan-Michael.html

Ramanathan, A. (n.d.). The power of failure: Michael Jordan's journey to success. LinkedIn. Retrieved from https://www.linkedin.com/pulse/power-failure-michael-jordans-journey-success-akshay-ramanathan

Greiveldinger, K. (n.d.). Learn how Michael Jordan overcame obstacles and you can too - Like a professional to win your day. Medium. Retrieved from https://keithgreiveldinger.medium.com/learn-how-michael-jordan-overcame-obstacles-and-you-can-too-like-a-professional-to-win-your-day-b14950e6075c

Wikipedia. (2023, April 4). Michael Jordan. Retrieved from https://en.wikipedia.org/wiki/Michael_Jordan

Ducksters. (n.d.). LeBron James. Retrieved from https://www.ducksters.com/sports/lebron_james.php

Biography.com. (n.d.). LeBron James. Retrieved from https://www.biography.com/athletes/lebron-james

Lakers Nation. (n.d.). LeBron James biography. Retrieved from https://lakersnation.com/lebron-james-biography/

PhoneBurner. (n.d.). 7 business lessons you can learn from LeBron James. Retrieved from https://www.phoneburner.com/blog/7-business-lessons-you-can-learn-from-lebron-james

TAC Sports. (n.d.). Lessons we can learn from LeBron James. Retrieved from https://tacsports.ca/lessons-we-can-learn-from-lebron-james/

Word on Fire. (n.d.). 10 life lessons from LeBron James. Retrieved from https://www.wordonfire.org/articles/fellows/10-life-lessons-from-lebron-james/

Bleacher Report. (n.d.). Ten reasons everyone loves LeBron James. Retrieved from https://bleacherreport.com/articles/435427-ten-reasons-everyone-loves-lebron-james

Leadership Excellence Now. (n.d.). Leadership lessons from LeBron James. Retrieved from https://leadershipexcellencenow.com/blog/leadership-lessons-from-lebron-james/

Britannica. (n.d.). Diana Taurasi. Retrieved from https://www.britannica.com/biography/Diana-Taurasi

USA Basketball. (n.d.). Diana Taurasi. Retrieved from https://www.usab.com/players/diana-taurasi

Wikipedia. (2023, April 4). Diana Taurasi. Retrieved from https://en.wikipedia.org/wiki/Diana_Taurasi

Simandan. (n.d.). Diana Taurasi: WNBA. Retrieved from https://www.simandan.com/diana-taurasi-wnba/

WNBA. (n.d.). Equality from basketball to the boardroom. Retrieved from https://mercury.wnba.com/news/equality-from-basketball-to-the-boardroom/

YouTube. (n.d.). [Video]. Retrieved from https://youtu.be/mfa0d25wEu8

Sports History Weekly. (n.d.). Magic Johnson & Larry Bird. Retrieved from https://www.sportshistoryweekly.com/stories/magic-johnson-larry-bird-la-lakers-boston-celtics-ncaa-march-madness,1133?

Mitchell & Ness Australia. (n.d.). Larry Bird vs. Magic Johnson. Retrieved from https://www.mitchellandness.com.au/articles/larry-bird-vs-magic-johnson

Yardbarker. (n.d.). Larry Bird perfectly explained how intense his rivalry with Magic Johnson was. Retrieved from https://www.yardbarker.com/nba/articles/larry_bird_perfectly_explained_how_intense_his_rivalry_with_magic_johnson_was/s1_16751_38420114

Reddit. (n.d.). Magic vs. Bird: Why did it revitalize the NBA?. Retrieved from https://www.reddit.com/r/nba/comments/s68w69/serious_magic_vs_bird_why_did_it_revitalize_the/

Anderson, C. (2019, December 27). Magic Johnson, Larry Bird, Lakers, Celtics: 40-year anniversary. Sports Illustrated. https://www.si.com/nba/2019/12/27/magic-johnson-larry-bird-lakers-celtics-40-year-anniversary

Wikipedia. (2023, April 4). Magic & Bird: A Courtship of Rivals. Retrieved from https://en.wikipedia.org/wiki/Magic_%26_Bird:_A_Courtship_of_Rivals

Lakers Nation. (n.d.). Kobe Bryant biography: Life, Lakers career, and legacy. Retrieved from https://lakersnation.com/kobe-bryant-biography-life-lakers-career-and-legacy/

Wikipedia. (2023, April 4). Kobe Bryant. Retrieved from https://en.wikipedia.org/wiki/Kobe_Bryant

Britannica. (n.d.). Kobe Bryant. Retrieved from https://www.britannica.com/biography/Kobe-Bryant

Foundation for Economic Education. (n.d.). Mamba mentality: The mindset that made Kobe Bryant a master. Retrieved from https://fee.org/articles/mamba-mentality-the-mindset-that-made-kobe-bryant-a-master/

Bryant, K. (2018). The Mamba Mentality: How I Play. MCD/Farrar, Straus and Giroux.

Wikipedia. (2023, April 4). Tim Duncan. Retrieved from https://en.wikipedia.org/wiki/Tim_Duncan

Moeller, C. (n.d.). Stick to your fundamentals: A Tim Duncan story. Retrieved from https://chadmoellerbaseball.com/stick-to-your-fundamentals-a-tim-duncan-story/

Fadeaway World. (n.d.). Tim Duncan: The biography of the Big Fundamental. Retrieved from https://fadeawayworld.net/nba/tim-duncan-the-biography-of-the-big-fundamental

Naismith Memorial Basketball Hall of Fame. (n.d.). Tim Duncan. Retrieved from https://www.hoophall.com/hall-of-famers/tim-duncan/

Biography.com. (n.d.). Stephen Curry. Retrieved from https://www.biography.com/athletes/stephen-curry

Wikipedia. (2023, April 4). Stephen Curry. Retrieved from https://en.wikipedia.org/wiki/Stephen_Curry

Yahoo Sports. (n.d.). Steph Curry reveals secret behind his shooting form. Retrieved from https://sports.yahoo.com/steph-curry-reveals-secret-behind-025218719.html

NBC Sports Bay Area. (n.d.). Steph Curry: The perfect combination of humble and arrogant. Retrieved from https://www.nbcsportsbayarea.com/nba/golden-state-warriors/steph-curry-the-perfect-combination-of-humble-and-arrogant/1180598/

Baron Rings. (n.d.). Exclusive look at Sue Bird's historical basketball career. Retrieved from https://baronrings.com/exclusive-look-at-sue-birds-historical-basketball-career/

Wikipedia. (2023, April 4). Sue Bird. Retrieved from https://en.wikipedia.org/wiki/Sue_Bird

Olympics. (n.d.). Basketball star Sue Bird retires: Titles, records, stats. Retrieved from https://olympics.com/en/news/basketball-star-sue-bird-retires-titles-records-stats

Olympics. (n.d.). Giannis Antetokounmpo: Origin story of a basketball legend. Retrieved from https://olympics.com/en/news/giannis-antetokounmpo-origin-story-basketball-legend

Wikipedia. (2023, April 4). Giannis Antetokounmpo. Retrieved from https://en.wikipedia.org/wiki/Giannis_Antetokounmpo

Lines. (n.d.). Giannis Antetokounmpo. Retrieved from https://www.lines.com/nba/players/giannis-antetokounmpo-497

Time. (2017). Giannis Antetokounmpo: American Voices 2017. Retrieved from https://time.com/collection/american-voices-2017/4624632/giannis-antetokounmpo-american-voices/

USOPM. (n.d.). Lisa Leslie: Achieving her basketball dream. Retrieved from https://usopm.org/lisa-leslie-achieving-her-basketball-dream/

National Women's History Museum. (n.d.). Lisa Leslie. Retrieved from https://www.womenshistory.org/education-resources/biographies/lisa-leslie

Wikipedia. (2023, April 4). Lisa Leslie. Retrieved from https://en.wikipedia.org/wiki/Lisa_Leslie

Wikipedia. (2023, April 4). Klay Thompson. Retrieved from https://en.wikipedia.org/wiki/Klay_Thompson

Fox Sports. (n.d.). Klay Thompson's grueling road back from two serious injuries. Retrieved from https://www.foxsports.com/stories/nba/klay-thompsons-grueling-road-back-from-two-serious-injuries

Sporting News. (n.d.). Klay Thompson injury timeline: Warriors return. Retrieved from https://www.sportingnews.com/us/nba/news/klay-thompson-injury-timeline-warriors-return/hos971zic7q01r7fanbxah52r

NBC Sports Bay Area. (n.d.). How overcoming injuries helped Klay learn the balance of life. Retrieved from https://www.nbcsportsbayarea.com/nba/golden-state-warriors/how-overcoming-injuries-helped-klay-learn-the-balance-of-life/1420140/

ESPN. (n.d.). Inside Klay Thompson's epic comeback. Retrieved from https://www.espn.com/nba/story/_/id/35027606/inside-klay-thompson-epic-comeback

Wikipedia. (2023, April 4). Jeremy Lin. Retrieved from https://en.wikipedia.org/wiki/Jeremy_Lin

The Ringer. (2022, February 4). Jeremy Lin, Linsanity, and the Knicks: Asian American representation 10 years later. Retrieved from https://www.theringer.com/nba2022/2/4/22916972/jeremy-lin-linsanity-knicks-asian-american-representation-10th-anniversary

NBC News. (n.d.). Jeremy Lin reflects on Linsanity 10 years later, gets candid about big regret. Retrieved from https://www.nbcnews.com/news/asian-america/jeremy-lin-reflects-linsanity-10-years-later-gets-candid-big-regret-rcna15364

Kiddle. (n.d.). Jeremy Lin. Retrieved from https://kids.kiddle.co/Jeremy_Lin

Chua, J. (2015, December 28). Before the Linsanity. The Atlantic. https://www.theatlantic.com/education/archive/2015/12/before-the-linsanity/625504/

Wikipedia. (2023, April 4). Wilt Chamberlain. Retrieved from https://en.wikipedia.org/wiki/Wilt_Chamberlain

Hoop Heaven. (2017, October). Wilt Chamberlain: A lasting legacy as a basketball legend and more. Retrieved from http://davidgarfieldshoopheaven.blogspot.com/2017/10/wilt-chamberlain-left-lasting-legacy-as.html

Bleacher Report. (n.d.). NBA: The case for Wilt Chamberlain as the best ever. Retrieved from https://bleacherreport.com/articles/1217186-nba-the-case-for-wilt-chamberlain-as-the-best-ever

The Philadelphia Inquirer. (n.d.). Wilt Chamberlain to LeBron James: NBA scoring record. Retrieved from https://www.inquirer.com/sixers/wilt-chamberlain-lebron-james-nba-scoring-record-20230208.html

Wikipedia. (2023, April 4). List of career achievements by Wilt Chamberlain. Retrieved from https://en.wikipedia.org/wiki/List_of_career_achievements_by_Wilt_Chamberlain

NBA. (n.d.). History: NBA legend Wilt Chamberlain. Retrieved from https://www.nba.com/news/history-nba-legend-wilt-chamberlain

Wikipedia. (2023, April 4). 2004 NBA Finals. Retrieved from https://en.wikipedia.org/wiki/2004_NBA_Finals

NBA. (n.d.). History: Top moments, Pistons shock NBA world, win championship in 2004. Retrieved from https://www.nba.com/news/history-top-moments-pistons-shock-nba-world-win-championship-in-2004

ClickOnDetroit. (2023, June 14). Today in history: '04 Pistons finish off Lakers to win 3rd NBA title. Retrieved from https://www.clickondetroit.com/sports/2023/06/14/today-in-history-04-pistons-finish-off-lakers-to-win-3rd-nba-title/

Yahoo Sports. (n.d.). Why the 2004 NBA champion Detroit Pistons are still so important. Retrieved from https://sports.yahoo.com/why-the-2004-nba-champion-detroit-pistons-are-still-so-important-211333308.html

Wikipedia. (2023, April 4). 2008 United States men's Olympic basketball team. Retrieved from https://en.wikipedia.org/wiki/2008_United_States_men%27s_Olympic_basketball_team

NBC Sports Chicago. (n.d.). Who played for the Redeem Team in the 2008 Olympics? Retrieved from https://www.nbcsportschicago.com/nba/chicago-bulls/who-played-for-the-redeem-team-in-2008-olympics/334105/

Olympics. (n.d.). What is the Redeem Team?. Retrieved from https://olympics.com/

en/news/what-is-the-redeem-team

People. (n.d.). Dwyane Wade talks Kobe Bryant and memories of the 2008 Redeem Team. Retrieved from https://people.com/sports/dwyane-wade-talks-kobe-bryant-and-memories-of-the-2008-redeem-team/

Printed in Great Britain
by Amazon

53402525R00076